WALKING WITH SOBONFU

A Guide to Claiming Your Authenticity and Deepening Your Sense of Community

SUSAN HOUGH

EMPOWER
P   R   E   S   S

An Imprint for GracePoint Publishing (www.GracePointPublishing.com)

GracePoint Matrix, LLC
322 N Tejon St. #207
Colorado Springs CO 80903
www.GracePointMatrix.com
Email: Admin@GracePointMatrix.com
SAN # 991-6032

ISBN-13: (Paperback) – 978-1-951694-63-0
eISBN: (eBook) – 978-1-951694-64-7

Library of Congress Control Number: 2021912276

Books may be purchased for educational, business, or sales promotional use.
For bulk order requests and price schedule contact:
Orders@GracePointPublishing.com

For more great books, please visit Empower Press online at
https://gracepointpublishing.com

I dedicate this book to my grandson, Paolo Zayn Hammad, who recently entered this world, and to Sobonfu Somé, who left us. And to my children, Ashley and Branner, who have always been my motivation to be a better person and grow and become who I am.

TABLE OF CONTENTS

Acknowledgments ix

From the Author xi

Introduction 1

   Ancient Application for Modern Times 1

Chapter 1 ~ Sobonfu's Way of Practice 7

   How Do I Pray by Sobonfu Somé 9

Chapter 2 ~ The Medicine Wheel 18

   The Dagara Tradition 18

Chapter 3 ~ Fire Element 23

   Fire/Ancestor Shrine 29

Chapter 4 ~ Water Element 36

   Water/Releasing Shrine 42

Chapter 5 ~ Earth Element 50

   Earth/Grounding Shrine 54

Chapter 6 ~ Mineral Element 60

   Mineral/Storytelling Shrine 65

Chapter 7 ~ Nature Element 70

   Nature/Plant and Animal Shrine 72

Chapter 8 ~ Walk with Endings 79

   Weaving All the Elements 85

Dagara Medicine Wheel 89

Workbook 93

   Aligning with Your Medicine Wheel 93

About the Author 107

Acknowledgments

Just like it takes a village to raise a child, it took a village to write this book. This book would not exist without the encouragement and kick in the pants from Jen Hutchinson who so strongly believed I had a story to tell, she started this book with me.

Thanks go to Jennifer Halls and Brian Fillman, who were with me from the beginning of my walking with Sobonfu and have stuck with me all this time. As well as my Ritual Village in Virginia, who came together to learn Sobonfu's teachings and have enriched my life ever since. Thank you to Judith Kent who helped me figure out what food goes with each element.

I give thanks to my West Coast villagers who have journeyed with me through the many iterations and revisions of this manuscript and also walked with me on the West Coast.

Thank you to my reviewers Kerri Consadori, Marcia Sargeant, Alan Sardella, Leonard Szymczak for their input and insight, and Katherine Prum for editing and formatting the book for submission to publication. Thanks to Anna Madorsky for her brilliant photography and Susan Brown for her artistic eye.

Thank you to Robert Strock who encouraged me to include in my writing the value in exposing my personal vulnerability as both genuine and as a key contribution to the teaching, which would have been hard to have done on my own. For that I am very proud and grateful.

.

FROM THE AUTHOR

This is a story about my journey with Sobonfu Somé. She is from a small village in Burkina Faso, West Africa, the Dagara tribe. I was honored to meet and learn from this woman for seventeen years. Her name means "keeper of the rituals," yet she was much more than that. She taught worldwide and helped thousands of people find their deeper calling and themselves. She was humble and believed that no one person was better than the next. She would never have called herself a guru or shaman.

Sobonfu spoke in small groups and large auditoriums all over the world. In fact, one time when I journeyed with her, she gave the opening prayer at Bringing the World Into Balance (May 29, 2003) and introduced Gloria Steinem, who said, "That woman changed me in fifteen minutes." Ms. Steinem didn't go any further than that about the encounter and continued her speech, speaking eloquently. I leaned over to Sobonfu and asked, "What did you say to her?" Her reply? "I don't have a freaking clue, maybe it was about rituals, I don't really know." That is who Sobonfu was. She taught without knowing it, carrying wisdom that changed people simply by being in her presence.

When I read Sobonfu's book I had a toddler and a ten-year-old in tow. I was feeling lost in my career at the time, feeling I needed something deeper. I had already been on a journey—checking out many alternative healing practices—and found all of it intriguing. I loved doing things that felt on the edge and have always loved people *and* needed a connection to something deeper. I just didn't know how to get the connection that worked for me. I needed a place to call home inside of me as well as on the outside. My searching, and every step along the way thus far, got me a little bit closer. It wasn't until Sobonfu that I really allowed Spirit to start talking to me in a fuller way. Her people, her ways, and the way she moved felt right, and then a new chapter of my story started to emerge.

I invite you to journey with me into this book and see how this story can awaken your gift and parts of you. Parts that have been asleep and are now ready to be called forth so you can bring your gift and your essence out more fully into the world.

INTRODUCTION

Ancient Application for Modern Times

Why is a white woman like me doing African rituals? Twenty-five years ago, I never would have thought I'd be doing anything like this. Yet, as I look back on my journey, I can see how my childhood played a part in my life traveling this path. As a preteen I always questioned everything in my life and believed strongly that it was all connected to something larger. I remember standing inside of the front door of my home and yelling at my mother to come quick: "Look! Jesus is talking to me. See the cross on the moon?"

She replied, "Open the door, Susan. It isn't a cross. It is the shadow of the screen."

"That's what you think," I replied.

Of course looking back I realize that I hadn't seen Jesus in the literal sense, but I had experienced him as an inner knowing. I was convinced that there was a deeper reason that we're alive than what I was being shown or taught. And while I didn't doubt what I believed, something stopped me from fully accepting my beliefs. As a result, I only started seeking my connection to the bigger picture a little later in life, when I was pregnant with my first child. Thankfully, I strongly believe my ancestors have pushed and shoved me all along the way, asking me to listen to that deeper calling inside of me.

I had a mentor and a teacher named David Davis. He was kind of a wizard king. A few months before he died, he told me, "You ought to read this book *The Spirit of Intimacy* written by Sobonfu Somé." I not only followed his suggestion, but I also read her second book *Welcoming Spirit Home*. That book touched my heart unlike any other, awakening something that I knew my heart and soul needed.

She wrote of the hearing ritual. When a woman becomes pregnant in the village, the villagers gather around her. The new spirit that is coming into the world speaks through its mother and tells the community its gift and what it is bringing to the community. The spirit also says what the child will need from the community to help them bring that gift to the village. This ritual felt so right to me it made me wish I had received a similar hearing ritual. I can imagine many of you may feel the same way.

Don't get me wrong. I was raised in a small community in Virginia, and I was blessed with a lot of support in my life. But, just imagine what it would be like to have your gift named, to be constantly reminded of it, and then have people support and nurture your uniqueness along the way. That's what drove me to seek out Sobonfu.

After I read Sobonfu's books, I felt ignited—a powerful, passionate, persistent, intuitive feeling burned within me. I couldn't stop thinking about her. I sensed my ancestors telling me to take this opportunity and run with it. The fire within pushed me to burn through obstacles and align myself to my passion. I kept talking to others about her books, yet it wasn't enough to just talk about them, I felt I had to *do* something.

After I read about the hearing ritual, I felt compelled to give her book to the people I loved. I gave away countless books to my closest and dearest friends—my community. Then I made them listen to me tell them how much I wanted to meet the author. My heart had been opened by her story and her village. I knew we needed to live differently, in community. It was missing from our lives.

Community is a part of me and who I am. My childhood was filled with cousins visiting my home and staying for the summers. My maternal grandmother lived with me all my life. I shared a room with her. My paternal granddaddy lived close by and visited every Sunday. I felt loved. My cousins spent summers with us and would be sent to my home if their parents were tired of them or thought they needed more "grandmother" time. My parents gave refuge to people from Vietnam and Poland to help them start a new life. If someone needed support they could always stay at our home. We had a revolving door of visitors and I loved it. The more people around, the happier I was. It's no wonder Sobonfu's village and upbringing woke me up to remembering the value of togetherness.

After driving people crazy with my love for Sobonfu's book, I searched the internet to find out where she was teaching. My fire had been so completely ignited that I had to talk to this woman. I had to bring her to my home to teach me and others. This desire to connect with her fueled my flames. The fire possessed me.

I eventually found a place in South Carolina where she was teaching. They gave me her phone number and I started calling her. When no one answered, I called again and again. Every once in a while, a woman would answer the phone and tell me that Sobonfu was traveling. As I hung up the phone, I wondered what kind of author doesn't have a fucking answering machine! I did this for nearly four months. I got so wound up that I called my friend Jennifer to complain that I still hadn't gotten an answer.

The fire kept burning and pushing me to persevere. Then one day, a woman with an African accent answered. Her first word was, "Yes." No hello, just a *yes*. Then, "I will do what you want, you can call my assistant."

"I don't even know what I want," I responded.

She gave me a number and the conversation was over. I had no idea what I wanted at the time, but I knew I had to meet this woman. I called her assistant and made arrangements to bring her to my hometown in Leesburg, Virginia. I didn't have a clue what I was getting myself into, but I didn't care. The fire was so strong I was willing to take the risk. The moment I met her, I felt a natural connection; it was a connection that altered the course of my life. Within a few months of meeting her, I became her assistant, helping her to organize workshops. I went from not knowing this woman at all, to speaking with her every single day. Sobonfu became a central part of my life.

Looking back, it seems obvious that my ancestors pushed me to connect with her. My decision to journey with Sobonfu is one of the best things I've ever done, equivalent—amazingly—to having my children. I am grateful that I listened to my inner voice. If I had not, I would never have walked with Sobonfu in this life, nor would I continue to walk with her now that she has transitioned to the other side. I am pretty sure she continues to push me and nudge me to do what I love in the world. I get to help others see their gifts, the ones only they can bring to the world in their own special way. I feel blessed to bring these teachings to you. Through the sale of this book I am also blessed to be able to bring water to the people I love in Burkina Faso, India, Kenya and in other indigenous villages. Thank you.

As I share my experience, I realize I have been deeply touched by this particular African teaching which happens to be common amongst Aboriginal tribes throughout the world. I realized that you might not have been exposed in this way. So even if various elements of these teachings might not be familiar to you (like my references to communicating with my ancestors or if you have never done rituals as a part of your practice), I encourage you to take in the essence of what I am conveying. It is perfectly understandable and natural when I make reference to having communication with my ancestors for you to perhaps think you might be communicating with your inner wisdom or some of the best parts of your spiritual teachings. I ask you, in your own language, to take the freedom of interpreting everything according to your life and not resist the way I experienced it or the way it is taught. I appreciate your need to stay with your own truth and your own methods and I ask you to treat what I am saying in the same way. I might be talking about walking with Sobonfu, yet you may interpret this as walking with Jesus, Mohammed, Moses, Buddha, or your present teacher. My wish is that you receive the benefit and wisdom and not to resist the details or methods of what is being presented.

For example, you might be oriented toward developing compassion and I might be writing about living our gifts. I may be talking about ancestors and you may understand that as aspects of faith or wisdom. At the most essential level it is important that we have our own approach to becoming wiser and more compassionate. The details will change depending on our culture, religion, or life experiences. We all need to do our best to see the essential similarities rather than fixate on our differences of approach.

As you read this book, walk with Sobonfu, her teachings, and me, so that you can awaken your gift and ignite your passion to share with the world. As she often said, "We are not meant to do this alone. We need to see that we are better together with our gifts. That is best done in community." I profoundly honor Sobonfu's path.

CHAPTER 1

Sobonfu's Way of Practice

*Community is the spirit, the guiding light of the tribe, whereby people
come together to fulfill a specific purpose, to help others fulfill their
purpose, and to take care of one another. The goal of community
is to make sure that each member is heard and is properly giving
the gifts he or she has brought to this world. Without this giving,
community dies. And without community, individuals are left without
a place where they can contribute. Community is that grounding
place where people share their gifts and receive from others.*

~ Sobonfu Somé

In the Dagara tradition, life is ritual. Everything—literally *everything*
from waking, cooking, and eating, to carrying water and, especially,
sleeping—is done with intention and in ritual. There are rituals for every
moment, every occasion, and every milestone. There are individual rituals,
maintenance rituals, radical rituals, and community rituals which involve
the elementals and our ancestors. All rituals begin with intention.

Intention is where you begin. It is the *Why!* Why are you here? Why
were you born? What is your gift? How would you like to change your past,
present, and future? It is about how you want to align yourself with your
purpose and dreams, how you want to be in relationship with yourself and
your community. Intention is making a connection with your Higher Self
and your soul's calling. It is the common denominator of every ritual. It
creates space to infuse meaning into your thoughts and actions.

As you read this book, my intention for you is to deepen your connection to Spirit, and to your gifts. It is to awaken and ignite a deeper connection to your dreams and the depth of who you are. It is to align with your heart's calling and deepen the love for yourself and others. My intention is that you can clearly see and release those patterns that have gotten in your way so you may awaken to remembering that you were born with a purpose, and that your gifts are needed. Lastly, it is so that you no longer walk alone, but that we walk in community.

HOW TO SET YOUR INTENTION

Setting intentions begins with centering yourself, quieting your mind, and focusing on your desire or goal. Your intention is your desire or goal whether you're conscious of it or not. For example, you may want to have a stronger connection with a loved one, a closer relationship with Spirit (or whatever you may want to call it), or maybe you want a new job. It could also be the goal to stop a pattern or bad habit. Or let go of the anger you're holding about a person or situation. Intention is the beginning of every ritual. It is always alright to change, adapt, and refocus your intention as you go along, especially as your desire or goals change.

Let's begin now with your setting intentions for reading this book. What is your intention at this moment? It can be wanting to see things from a new vantage point, or helping you connect to a deeper healing. It can be wanting to know yourself better or awaken to a greater self-love. Maybe your intention is to wake up and find your fire. As you read this book, take the time to set and define your intention; over time, reset and redefine. You have permission to change your mind. There are no rules. Intentions are always changing in response to your circumstances, feelings, mood, or environment.

WHAT IS RITUAL?

In Sobonfu's words, a ritual is "a ceremony in which we call in Spirit to be the driving force, the overseer of our activities... Dagara rituals are about healing, an acknowledgement of people and their gifts, and making Spirit visible or tangible." (excerpted from *Welcoming Spirit Home*, 2009)

In my words, ritual is taking action when you want to shift, to move out of your head and into your heart. It's not passive. It's an opportunity to deepen your connection to yourself, your community, and your purpose. It can remove blocks and awaken you to your true self.

WHAT IS PRAYER?

Prayer helps frame your intention for the ritual. It's a conversation between you and Spirit to bring in the most compassionate energy to support your life. Talk to Spirit like you talk to your friends, but even more authentically. Be yourself. If you need to scream at Spirit, scream at Spirit. If you feel gratitude, let yourself really feel it. Get grounded, tap into your emotions. Be authentic with Spirit. You don't have to play nice. Be real with Spirit. Prayer is not about playing nice.

HOW DO I PRAY? By Sobonfu Somé

I pray in many different ways
The clarity of my intention is the beginning of my prayer.
In my tradition every breath I draw is a prayer.
Every time I inhale and exhale it is a prayer.
So how conscious are you when you are breathing in and out?
How conscious are you when you are walking?
How conscious are you when you are singing?
How conscious are you when you are angry?
I pray in the way I show gratitude, love, or compassion.
I pray alone and in community.
I pray with my thoughts.
I pray with my body.
I pray in the way I speak to people.
I pray to the various elements of nature — the trees, the animals, the
*   water, the rocks, the earth, the fire. . .*
I pray to the ancestors and all the Divinities.
I pray simply with passion, humility, clarity, and grace.
I pray in the way I welcome and bless people.
I pray with whatever emotions come my way.
I pray with sincerity and strong belief that what I am praying for is going
*   to manifest.*
In my tradition whatever you say is a prayer that you send out,

Because sound is a powerful force that brings the hidden to light.
And when you pray, something is going to say yes.
So each moment in my life is a prayer.
Each moment I reflect on myself, on the world, and on other people is a
   prayer.
How I interact with people and how I deal with my thoughts is a prayer.
How genuine am I—is a way for me to pray.
For me all these things are sacred and are messengers, and can take my
   heart cries, which are my prayers to the Divinities.
This is the power of how I pray.

INITIATION TO LOST BUT VITAL RITUALS

In 2004, I traveled with Sobonfu and a group of eleven other people to her village in Burkina Faso, West Africa to dig a well for her community. Most of us had traveled together from Virginia, and all of us had been involved in one way or another with Sobonfu's training. We were between the ages of fifteen and sixty-five years old, and were all excited to experience her way of communal living. As we left Ouagadougou, the capital of Burkina Faso, I became excited about finally leaving the city and trekking to her village. As we headed out, I couldn't help but compare this hot, dirty, sandy desert, that had no available water sources and very little color, to my homeland, which was the complete opposite with its lush green colors.

Sobonfu told us that in her tribe, there is no social ranking or hierarchy. Everyone is equal and everything is shared. Women cook together and, in the mornings, they walk together with their children to get water, together. They build their homes communally, sing while building the homes, and sleep together. They are even quiet together. Men do the same. They hunt together and build together. The whole community eats together.

Dagara culture is communal. It is just their way of being. Their boundaries are different from the West. Nothing is *yours* or *mine*; everything is *ours*. They even share their clothes. Sobonfu used to say she wasn't sure whose clothes she would bring home with her. One time when she was traveling, Sobonfu saw a woman who lived in a village hours away, wearing her coat. She didn't feel upset by this at all. She said, "We share, and whoever needs an item is the one who is using it at any given moment." Every time I cherish and remember this way of living it reminds me of John Lennon's song "Imagine." Can you imagine that?

She also told us the village didn't keep feelings secret. If a woman is struggling, so are her sisters. Women tend to one another, always conscious of what each other needs. If someone is too quiet, she won't be allowed to remain that way for long. Every woman is a sister and notices if something is wrong. If a woman isn't ready to talk—good luck. Her sisters will make her speak about what is troubling her. And they'll call in others to create a space to help her release whatever needs to be resolved. I realized I was going to fit in really well in the village. I was aware of a life longing that I hadn't been able to put into words. It made me understand at yet another level why I had wanted to meet Sobonfu so badly. I have always wanted to speak absolutely freely—a desire that would seem like the most natural act in the world. And yet, in our Western society, I had always felt a little bit crazy for wanting it. Hearing Sobonfu explain the workings of her village brought incomparable joy and relief at the same time.

Weddings in the village are a community event. Not only does the couple say their vows, but every other couple renews their vows at the same time. Unless you are from the village, it's impossible to figure out whose wedding you are attending. When one couple gets married, everyone gets married. Even unmarried people make a commitment to the couple as well as themselves. A wedding day is a day of celebration for everyone.

The same is true with grief. If you are in the village and experience a loss of some kind, you do not go through it alone. "This is normal," Sobonfu would say, "We live communally and are always available for one another."

I didn't truly understand it at first. This wasn't how I was brought up. As I grew up, I learned to be self-reliant and independent. I had forgotten what it was like to share a home, clothes, food, thoughts, even grief. In fact, in my home, it would make my sister angry if she caught me wearing her clothes without permission. And any talk of struggle would be shared only within the family, if discussed at all. My dad struggled if we cried and would say something like, "I'll give you something to cry about." But Sobonfu offered another way. She said that every person has a gift that they bring to the village. Each gift is what the village needs to survive and thrive.

Two days before leaving the capital, Sobonfu took me and the others to see a water diviner. The other travelers had loved the experience. I, on the other hand, felt perturbed and frustrated with my encounter.

The thin elder water diviner came to Sobonfu's brother's home to meet with us. Sobonfu acted as interpreter during our sessions. He held a calabash gourd full of water and asked me to hold it, then breathe into the water. After I did this, he looked into the water and spoke to Sobonfu about what he saw. Excited, I waited to hear what he had to say about me and my family. He had spent considerable time giving his reading to the others, who had come back excited, longing to do the rituals he had given to them to clear out and support them in their growth and inner knowing. I anticipated the same happy, positive reading. As it turned out, while he did say a few things about my children, when he started to talk about me, he said very little.

Sobonfu told me he had said, "You need to do a betrayal ritual." Of course that made sense! My ex-husband had definitely betrayed me. It was painfully obvious what he was talking about—while my husband's actions had hurt me deeply, I still hadn't accepted the part I had played in the relationship. Beyond this, the elder didn't elaborate. He said he would tell me more after I completed the ritual. I felt disappointed. I just wanted to get the ritual over with. I kept asking Sobonfu when I could do my ritual. She kept replying, "Not yet."

At first, I felt okay that I wasn't allowed to do my ritual immediately. But after days of Sobonfu refusing me while the others were able to do their rituals, I felt more and more annoyed at both her and the process.

I still had not completed my ritual as we finally traveled to Sobonfu's village. Twelve of us squeezed into a van with no air-conditioning. The temperature was 120 degrees outside. Chickens stored under the seat nipped at my toes. I wore a surgical mask to keep the dust out of my nose. Sweat dripped down my face. I was hot, agitated, and disgruntled because I wanted to complete my ritual. Pressed into the van with everyone, baking and aggravated, I asked Sobonfu, "Can I do my ritual now?"

She continued to say, "Not yet."

With every mile I became increasingly frustrated. I suddenly felt a hot wave of energy come over me which wasn't from the steaming van. Sweltering in that moment, I realized all the ways I had betrayed myself in allowing my ex-husband to treat me badly. I had pretended my life was good at the time when I actually knew I was being betrayed. I knew he was not being faithful and I was betraying myself by staying mostly in denial and continuing to try to please him. I knew I had betrayed myself by not speaking up.

I betrayed *myself.* The real healing could only occur when I was willing to be honest about the part I played in this failed marriage. I felt this amazing sense of flow through my entire being: a sense of calm and peace and inner knowing emerged as I awakened to my own betrayal. With that opening and realization, tears poured down my face. I understood how I had played the victim of my own life.

At that moment, almost unbelievably, without talking to her or seeing me in the back seat, Sobonfu turned around and said, "Now you can do your betrayal ritual." She had the driver pull over and motioned for me to get out of the van and do my ritual. I spotted a homeless man and gave him a t-shirt and bread in a way prescribed by the elder. My heart opened even more. Healing flowed through my body. It felt like pieces of my spirit that had been lost when I betrayed myself, started to come back together. As I became reunited with myself, I felt overwhelmed with joy. I was finally able to start to forgive my ex-husband on a whole different level.

After I did the ritual, I got back into the van, feeling a deeper connection to myself and everyone around me. I had an experience that left me confident that I could be less resentful with my ex-husband and could practice what I had learned in Africa with those around me in the West.

We continued our journey, eventually turning off the main highway. There was no real road, and even if it was bumpy and uncomfortable, it was obviously the way. I, however, felt more at peace than I had since my ex-husband had betrayed me. My heart was open.

All of a sudden, boys on rusty, beaten-up bicycles appeared in front of the van. They motioned to us and told Sobonfu we couldn't drive any further. We got out and started walking up a hill. At first, I heard faint sounds, but as we approached the top of the hill, I saw 600 people singing and dancing, filled with joy. The energy of the singing moved me unlike anything I had ever felt before—as if my soul was awakening, remembering who I was. My body filled with exuberance and joy. I didn't understand why; I only knew that I felt welcomed and at home for the first time. With all this energy coming my way, I started sobbing.

I finally said to Sobonfu, "Is this because we're bringing water to the village?"

"No, honey. When someone leaves the village and comes home, people gather to welcome them back." My heart opened even wider. I had never felt that welcomed by people whom I didn't know. For the first time, I felt a deeper sense of being at home with myself. I felt taken in and honored for just showing up. Now I truly understood the meaning of community.

Sobonfu always said welcoming was the one ritual we need to perform in Western culture. We don't take the time to welcome each other, to truly see that everyone is a gift to the world. The welcoming helps us remember the gifts we each carry and gives us the opportunity to see how necessary we each are to the community. As Sobonfu repeated over and over again, "You are not an accident. You are a well, healthy, powerful being who has chosen to bring something unique into the world."

As I reflect on the magnitude and power of the Welcoming Ritual, with its community-wide sharing of all gifts, including clothes, food, and everything else, I realize that's exactly the spirit in which I want to welcome you into the pages of this book. My prayer and Sobonfu's prayer for you is that as you read, you welcome your spirit home and awaken to your gifts you carry within you. May you feel embraced by spirit and know you are here for a reason.

WELCOMING THE DAY RITUAL

Sobonfu taught me this simple ritual to do every morning to welcome yourself back from the dreamtime. This ritual grounds you for the day ahead. As you wake up, before you do anything else, wrap your arms around yourself. Call in God or Spirit, your Higher Self or whatever it is that you most revere—the trust that guides you to your heart. Allow yourself to really feel loved as much as you can. Ask whomever you are calling upon to surround you and walk with you throughout the coming day, and help you awaken to loving yourself too. You may also say a prayer to focus your energy. You can use the following, or simply say whatever is most meaningful to you:

I call upon Spirit, who walks beside me, who knows me best, and knows what I need to support my Highest Self throughout this day. I am grateful to the Dreamworld, where we meet, for the sleep and information that has moved through me in the Dreamtime. Open me to hearing your messages throughout this day and aligning me to best serve you and do your work in the world. Thank you for the courage to be true to myself even when I'm afraid. May I listen to you and those around me with a loving, grounded heart.

Imagine your day unfolding as easily and lovingly as possible. Do this every day to connect with and allow love in more and more. Know that each day is a blessing and so are you. Once you have welcomed yourself to the day, take a moment to write down your dreams, if you remember them. If not, write down how you are feeling about the day ahead.

If you wake up feeling fearful, scared, or worried about something you received from your dreams, go outside under a tree and make a small circle with sacred ash from a wood fire or incense stick that you have prepared or been given. As you make the circle, talk about the dream and how you would like the dream to be changed so that it can bring peace to you and your family. Take a moment and pray to your higher self to turn the dream around and bring protection to you and to those you love. Pour a small amount of water in the middle of the ash circle you have created to represent bringing peace to the dream. Then as you come back inside, make a straight horizontal line with the ash across the threshold, repeating the prayer to turn around the dream, and bring peace to you and your family. As you pray, add a small drop of water in the middle of the line you drew with ash.

COMING HOME FROM YOUR DAY RITUAL

Choose a tree, a plant, a rock, or a water fountain near or at the entrance to your home. As you approach your home at the end of your day, touch the object and thank its spirit for helping you release whatever burdens or struggles from your day before you cross the threshold. Give gratitude for the day you've had. Once a week clean or care for whatever you've chosen (water the plant, refill the fountain, leave a token of food by the tree or rock) and again thank it for taking your crap.

You can also place the object (rock, plant, water feature) inside the door of your home. As you cross the threshold, say, "Hello, I'm home!" and set your intention that as you walk through the door you leave your emotional baggage from your day behind. Again touch the object with the intention that you enter freed from your worries and ready for a fresh start.

WELCOMING YOUR LOVED ONE RITUAL

This ritual can be done in your own home with your family and friends. When a loved one comes to see you or comes home from their day, stop whatever you are doing, if only for a moment. Greet them by saying, "Welcome home" along with their name. Show them how happy you are to have them in your home before you continue the rest of your evening. They may not realize how special this one moment is, but over time, it will make them feel more at home with you and within themselves. Sobonfu said that helping people feel welcomed is one of the most important gifts you can give your loved ones. Taking the time to welcome those you love throughout the day helps them feel more connected to their spirit, their gift, and to their community.

Imagine how beautiful it would be if you and your partner took the time to welcome each other with care. How do you think this ritual of welcoming would support you both by giving and receiving it? This is a question that I believe we could ask ourselves often as it will help us to remember.

CHAPTER 2

The Medicine Wheel

THE DAGARA TRADITION

We have five different elements: Earth, Water, Mineral, Fire, and Nature. The element Earth is responsible for our groundedness, our sense of identity, and our ability to nurture and to support one another. Water is peace, focus, wisdom, and reconciliation. Mineral helps us to remember our purpose and gives us the means to communicate and to make sense out of what others are saying. Fire is about dreaming, keeping our connection to the self and ancestors and keeping our visions alive. Nature helps us to be our true self, to go through major changes and life-threatening situations. It brings magic and laughter.

~ Sobonfu Somé

When I first started studying with Sobonfu, I didn't really understand what she was talking about when she said we were going to do "Elemental Rituals." I knew I wanted to know what they were, and something inside me told me to move out of my own way and give it a try. At this time in my life, I was driven to find my path. I knew one thing I wanted to reclaim was my relationship with Spirit/God. I also knew I needed to give my children a spiritual connection too. I wanted them to not feel alone in this world, and to believe there is more to life than just what we can see. I wanted my children to have community too, which my parents had created through their spiritual connection. Although traditional Christianity didn't fit for me, as a child the church provided me with a sense of belonging to something bigger than my immediate family. Being raised as a Christian gave me a love for God/Jesus, but Christianity felt too confining and too judgmental. I also resented that construct of being a sinner and therefore, not good enough. I struggled with people telling me who Jesus was, rather than being allowed my own interpretation of who Jesus is to me.

We all live such separate and isolated lives in this culture; we have forgotten what it is to live interdependently. Rituals bring us together. What I love about practicing Elemental Rituals in community is that they awaken those aspects inside ourselves and support our seeing how we are connected to everything. In this book, you will be introduced to Elemental Rituals, which are maintenance rituals for daily or weekly use or when needed. These rituals carry power and are ones you can start with and do on your own. There are others, called Radical Rituals, which I have been trained in, but won't be in this book because they require a mentor to guide and community to support you through the experience.

Rituals bring us together in awareness of our connection to the five elements of the Dagara Medicine Wheel: Fire, Water, Earth, Mineral, and Nature. This connection isn't dependent but is *inter*dependent. In western culture, dependency has a negative connotation. When experienced in a healthy way, in community, we are able to see that it allows us to be stronger, independent individuals. When did we, as a culture, decide that living alone in our little boxes and detached homes was healthy? It is not. It is isolating.

The elements and rituals that Sobonfu taught me helped—and continue to help—me open up. They created a deepening of intimacy and connection within myself, as well as others. Ritual practice provided a medium to connect in a more intimate way with my community. A healthy community creates space for people to hold each other in the experience of struggles and joys with authenticity, honesty, and truthfulness.

In Sobonfu's tradition, the elements are just as powerful as humans. In fact, they are part of your everyday life. We can become more and more aligned with them. All too often, "modern" people forget how to connect to those elements that are outside of us and those elements that lie within us. In this book, I will introduce you to each element in the medicine wheel. The description of each element will give you a different energy and feeling. Consider the Fire Element: it is warm, it is courage, it is light, it is the dream world, and it is our connection to Spirit and our ancestors. We each have a gift, and we need our connection to others in order to express it in the world. In our culture now, we often feel envious or jealous of what other people have. Other people have exactly what they need, and so do we. We are all better when we use our gifts together.

As our world has evolved, many of us have stopped recognizing and living in our relationship with the elements; all too often we have stopped feeling connected to each other. When you feel the support of the elements and connection to your community, your esteem naturally rises. You no longer feel as alone in the world or disconnected from your purpose. Let your own relationship with the elements start to expand as you read these pages.

SHRINES

In the Dagara tradition, there are shrines everywhere and you don't even know it. They are very simple, as simple as a mound of dirt. Daily life is centered around shrines and the acknowledgement of their connection to Spirit. They are essential to village life, representing a place to go to receive energy and connect to Spirit.

We combine the shrines with the elements of the medicine wheel to practice rituals that support daily life. Each shrine and ritual will be addressed with its corresponding element.

Throughout the rest of this book, I am going to focus on each of the Dagara elements one at a time and share my personal experiences with them. Here is a brief description of each element (more detail can be found in the workbook at the end of this book). We each incorporate all the elements within us, with one dominant element based on our birth year—to determine your personal element, reference the workbook.

FIRE: You use FIRE to connect to your ancestors. Remember ancestors can be Jesus, Buddha, your grandmother, as well as your best friend who passed away. They are your Fire. You use FIRE in your practice to IGNITE your PASSION and burn away what's in the way of your VISION and INTUITION. FIRE drives you to do and to dream. Too much FIRE, and you'll tend to act too quickly. Not enough FIRE, and you may procrastinate or get lost in self-doubt. FIRE allows you to align with your light.

WATER: You use WATER to help you find your FLOW—the BALANCE between what you take in and the ability to RELEASE what no longer serves you. WATER is all about peace and harmony. WATER brings clarity into your life. WATER helps you feel your feelings. It helps you get in touch with your feelings and helps you open to what those feelings are telling you. It helps you feel and release grief; it deepens your connection to yourself and Spirit. WATER brings FIRE into balance. It allows you to slow down.

EARTH: You use EARTH to get the NOURISHMENT you need. It is your soul food. EARTH allows you to hear and speak from your heart. EARTH grounds you and helps you to be more present in your body and provides a grounded sense of love. EARTH helps you feel at home in your body. Earth also shows you the gifts you are here to find and claim.

MINERAL: You use MINERAL to align with the real [remove: gift and] STORY of who you are. What story do you need to let go of and what story are you bringing into the world? MINERAL is about inner wisdom. Minerals/stones/rocks/bones help you to remember the stories from all lifetimes, our DNA, and help you to bring those stories into this lifetime to awaken the stories that came before you so they can be brought forward now. Minerals help you communicate with clarity. We carry the stories of our ancestors and the Wisdom of All Time in our bones and when we connect with rocks and stones, they help us to remember the stories and to shift and align with the stories within our own bones. Minerals help you release your patterns to become free to live your gifts.

NATURE: You use NATURE to bring transformation and CHANGE. It allows your true NATURE to come into balance. It allows you to see that life is constantly changing. It helps you to take off your mask and be your authentic self. NATURE helps you connect with MAGIC. Magic is the extraordinary in the ordinary that speaks to the human spirit, soul, and heart. It's the trickster, the fairy element, the ever-changing aspects of Nature that bring play and joy into your life. It lightens the mood when things get too heavy. Don't worry if you haven't experienced this too much because most people haven't. This illumination will help you bring this lightness forward in your life.

CHAPTER 3

Fire Element

*Ancestors are also referred to as spirits. The spirit of an
ancestor has the capacity to see not only into the invisible
spirit world but also into this world, and it serves as our
eyes on both sides. It is this power of ancestors that will help
us direct our lives and avoid falling into huge ditches.*

~ Sobonfu Somé

Born in Leesburg, Virginia, I was raised in a small, close-knit community by my parents, grandparents, and neighbors. I married, divorced,
and brought up my two children there, working in the mental health
field for twenty years. When I remarried at age fifty-three, I moved 3,000
miles across America to Laguna Beach, California.

At that time, I left my business which provided healing sessions to clients
by blending my mental health education with life coaching, energy healing,
and indigenous African wisdom practices. I said goodbye to the healing community that had taught me how to practice energy work, a community that had
nourished me, and where my ancestors resided. I left the fathers of my children,
my life-long friends, my parents' friends, and pretty much everything I knew.

This was an indescribably difficult period for me—I was battling breast
cancer, having just finished chemo and radiation treatments, I was struggling
with horrific nerve pain, and on top of that my mother had just passed away.
At the time, everything felt like an agonizing blur. And now I was taking a leap
of faith expecting to heal without all those people and the spirit of the place I

loved and called home. But I knew that I needed a new beginning, and the fact that Sobonfu lived in California was a good enough reason to move closer to her.

Before the move, I started talking to my ancestors, asking them for help with this new transition in my life. I wanted to bring my son to an area that supported him, and I was concerned that it would be hard for his father and him to be so far apart from one another. Once in our new home, feeling the loss of my community and needing to find my bearings, one of the first things I did was unpack my family pictures and set up my ancestor shrine. I carefully unwrapped and hung each one. I prayed they would help me to become grounded, and navigate my new surroundings. I prayed that my son would feel enough at home and would still feel supported and be resilient in the face of all these changes. I prayed he would remain connected to his father.

Through my initiation with Sobonfu, I learned the value of speaking to my ancestors and listening to my higher self. Whenever I am struggling, either emotionally or in any situation, I call them in and ask for their support. This has created a place within me where I can find companionship and feel less alone. Talking with my ancestors has become a way of life for me. I sit with them and have them work with me when I see clients, feel alone, and even when I am experiencing joy.

Sobonfu always said, "You must acknowledge those who come before you. Our ancestors see more clearly from the other side about what has worked and what hasn't worked for each of us and our lineage. They also see and know how to help you heal those lineage patterns." In the Dagara tradition into which I was initiated, ancestors are treated as a part of our still-living family, and so we honor them by including them as a living presence in our home. Even deeper than that though, in this tradition, our ancestors and guides are responsible for keeping us connected to who we really are and why we are here.

We learn that, even if we didn't like them in this lifetime, even if there were painful issues and strained relationships, once on the other side, it is their "job" to work with you to heal the family patterns and wounds they left behind. They feel responsible for not cleaning up their messes when they were alive, leaving them for you to fix. They want to be called upon now to support you in changing the lineage patterns they were unable to change.

I talk to my ancestors and Spirit like I would a close, intimate friend. I get real and honest with them and myself. This is different from how I was raised as a child in the Lutheran church. Back then, I believed that God was so big that the only thing I could talk to him about was how I messed up, what I did wrong, and what I needed. I was always asking for forgiveness. I didn't know then that if I connected to God, Spirit, or my ancestors, I could simply be myself and talk about everything that was on my mind. I could truly make them my friends instead of feeling separate and alone in this world. I know now that they are with me always. I just need to ask them to be there.

My father had always loved red cardinals and collected them. He even had little statues of them around his house. We shared this love of birds and would spend time observing all the birds on my back porch, and commenting on which ones were our favorites. Soon after he died, Sobonfu and I were standing in the kitchen in Virginia when I noticed a particular cardinal. I had never seen it before my dad died. This one had an odd beak and would appear when I was feeling lonely, worried, or grieving about my dad. Whenever I needed support or felt unsure, I would look out the window and see a flash of red fly in to rest on the branch of the tree in the yard. Sobonfu told me she knew that the red cardinal was my dad letting me know he was with me and supporting me. I felt protected and watched over and this allowed me to remain connected to my roots and my lineage.

There aren't any cardinals in Southern California. And living in my new home wasn't easy. I missed that red bird with its ugly beak, and wondered if I had made the right decision to move. As time went by, I still felt alone, unmoored in unchartered territory, frustrated, scared, and homesick. I really needed to feel the presence of my ancestors, especially my mom and dad. I questioned them silently: *Where are you? And why aren't you making yourselves known? Did I upset you by moving away? Can't you find me in California?*

My marriage had become difficult, and I felt isolated and powerless without my community around me. Fortunately, two of my closest friends, Brian and Cynthia, came to visit me in California. They had nurtured me through my sickness and graduated from the Ritual Healing Village with me. They knew me so deeply, I didn't have to tell them how homesick, how soul-sick, I was without them and my community. I prayed with them and did a ritual. I got down and dirty with Spirit. I was angry that I didn't know what my ancestors were thinking since I'd been living in California and didn't feel they had my back. I cried and raged at Spirit and my ancestors. My two friends held space for me to let out my feelings and to speak from my heart. This was also part of Sobonfu's teaching.

"Tell people how you feel," she told me. "You need family and friends to hold space for you to feel your feelings so you can be transformed. Don't hold feelings in and pretend you are okay when you aren't."

Brian and Cynthia listened to me share my struggle and pain. After I let go of the grief, I felt relief and renewed hope.

I asked them, "Can you help me figure out what to do?"

"Let's go take a walk on the beach," suggested Cynthia. "Remember how we used to go to the Potomac together and talk to our ancestors? We'll help you; we'll talk to them together, now."

We did just that. We went to the beach. We prayed. The waves crashed. Seagulls soared overhead on the fresh, clean ocean breeze that caressed our faces. Standing there with my friends, with members of my community, I felt more soul-nourished than I had in a long, long time. And honestly, that might have been enough to lift my spirits enough to keep on going.

But as I turned to go home—my new home—I immediately stopped in my tracks. Lying in the sand at my feet were two pieces of driftwood. One had a red tinge to it and looked like someone had carved a bird out of the wood, leaving a distinctly unique shape of a cardinal. I held it up and yelled to my friends. "My dad. It's my dad!" I was so excited; I didn't notice what else was there.

Brian said, "Susan, look down."

Lying next to the bird driftwood was a long, perfect stick in the shape of a wand, like the ones from Harry Potter. My mom's name was Wanda!

I started crying. My prayers had been answered. Both parents showed up. They had my back. And they were with me in California.

Whenever I tell that story, I feel deep gratitude to my ancestors. We are never walking alone. Messages and signs appear from the other side. When we choose to see them and start talking honestly to those who have come before us, they will show us they are always with us.

So call upon those who have gone before you. Those who love and know you and want to support you in this life. Breathe in that energy of love, warmth, and connection. Even if your ancestors weren't loving and wronged you while on the earth, they are now Spirit and want to make their wrongs right.

Sobonfu said, "Ancestors can see clearly once they have gone into the Spirit world again and show up to help you make right what they did wrong. Speak honestly to them about your fears, your trials, and, yes, even your gratitude. Make Spirit and your ancestors your friends. Make friends with others in the physical form, those who can support you in your struggles. Then see what unfolds."

As Sobonfu taught me, we are never alone even when we think we are. The Fire element is not just about our connection to the spirit world but it is also about our dreams. If you are a member of the Fire clan, you are in the elemental group that interprets dreams for the villagers. You also give them rituals if their dreams contain a concern or warning.

When I realized I was a part of the Fire clan, it made sense to me. Ever since I was a small girl my dreams told me information or at least allowed me to escape into another world of adventure. It wasn't unusual for me to have a dream that would then be confirmed when the event came true. In fact, I used to call Sobonfu when a dream concerned me, and many times she gave me a ritual to possibly turn around a nightmare. She had me re-visualize the dream and then either imagine the dream as I wanted it to be or cultivate certain qualities that were necessary to find strength, safety, peace, wisdom, or whatever was needed to turn it around. If it was one that I thought meant harm was coming to me or my loved ones, I would do a ritual with ash immediately to try and make the dream turn out in a positive way.

My father didn't just appear to me as a cardinal after he died in 2007. About a week before that first Christmas without him he appeared in a dream. The Christmas season was always a magical time with my dad. He thought through the presents that he gave us, taking care to make sure we liked them. My mom was the opposite, buying my sister and me matching sweaters which — shockingly — neither of us liked! The closer Christmas came, the sadder I felt that he was no longer going to spend Christmas morning with me or my children enjoying our holiday rituals. I remember going to bed wondering what I could do for my children and Mom to instill the same joy of Christmas that year.

Right before my alarm went off, I dreamt that I heard a phone ring and I answered it. On the other end I heard my father say, "This is your father, Roger Hough."

I know it's odd, but that is how he always spoke on the phone, addressing me as if I didn't recognize his voice. I said "Hi Dad," only then realizing he wasn't alive anymore. In the dream, I asked "Why are you calling me? You are dead."

He said, "I just wanted you to know I am doing well and that things are good on this side." He then said, "Don't forget to get something from me for the kids that they will like." We said our goodbyes. It wasn't an unusual conversation for me to have with him. He never stayed on the phone long. He was always very to the point.

I then woke up and realized that it had been a dream. I knew my dad had come to me. It was so real and so wonderful. I called Sobonfu afterward and she said, "Of course he showed up. He is always with you. Keep communication open. Ask him to enter your dreams and your waking world. Talk to him about your desires and sadness. Just because he is on the other side, it doesn't mean you can't communicate. You will just have to renegotiate your relationship to see how to do it and how to interpret what he wants to tell you. In fact your ancestors may not show up like mine. They will do it their own unique way with you. They could come with a smell or a sound."

My mother comes to me in a completely different way. Right before she died, I had taken her for a ride to her family home. I said, "Mom will you let me know that you are okay once you get to the other side?"

"Yes," she responded, "I will blow a horn so loud that you will stop in your tracks."

At my mother's funeral, when I got up to give her eulogy, one of my closest friend's car horn went off, and she couldn't get it to stop. Her keys were somehow locked in her car. Sobonfu, who was standing by me, whispered to me, "I guess your mom's doing just fine on the other side." It was the perfect confirmation to me. So remember, keep your eyes and ears open and trust that your ancestors can give you signs if you ask, and then take the time to listen.

Sobonfu taught this to me: Ancestors and Spirit want to come and live in your home with you! They want to eat with you and greet you in the morning. They want to send you messages in wood, stone, and song. Very simply put, they want a two-way conversation.

Sobonfu tells us that your relationship with Spirit and your ancestors should be the most intimate relationship in your life. Not Western intimate—African intimate, or *in-to-me-see* (intimacy). When you have this kind of relationship, its purpose is to constantly reflect back to you and keep you connected to who *you* really are. Spirit sees *you* so *you* can see *yourself.*

Now you're ready for the Fire element, which represents your connection to Spirit, your ancestors, your own light, your vision, your passions, and your dreams. When you hear the word *ritual*, I'm not talking about a magic spell. I prefer Sobonfu's description of ritual in *Welcoming Spirit Home.* "Ritual is a ceremony in which we call in Spirit to be the driver, the overseer of our activities. The elements of ritual allow us to connect with the self, the community, and the natural forces around us. In ritual, we call in our higher selves to show us obstacles that we cannot see because of our limitations as human beings. Rituals help us to remove blocks standing between our true spirit and ordinary humanness" (2009, 24).

Ritual is really as much about creating sacred space, like prayer or meditation, that's designed to get you out of your head space and emotional reactions and into your heart/soul space. That's where the magic of healing and transformation happens.

When we are in this humanness, we are analyzing, "should-ing," trying, assuming, and guessing. When we are in our heart/soul space, we are finding the frequency of Spirit that's waiting to send us a download through that now *open* channel.

FIRE/ANCESTOR SHRINE

The Fire shrine honors your ancestors, so we call it the ancestor shrine. Fire is the element that connects you to your ancestors. There is a specific way to create a fire shrine and it is done in a ritualistic way. It is among the most important rituals in the Dagara tradition and the foundation of every other ritual. The ancestor/fire shrine is the place to talk to your deceased loved ones, teachers, and all the spirits who support you.

The Ancestor shrine is a perpetual flame.

REASONS YOU USE A FIRE SHRINE:

- ➤ Communicate with your ancestors (or at least with the voice of your Higher Self or a spirit you feel close to) and find a friendly voice that might be your wisdom
- ➤ Ask for guidance, support, help, relief
- ➤ Pray to release anger, grief, sadness, heartache, worries
- ➤ Ask support for your vision and purpose
- ➤ Burn free from patterns and lineage karma
- ➤ Ignite your passions
- ➤ Open up to the dream world

TOOLS FOR THE FIRE/ANCESTOR SHRINE

- • Smudge stick
- • Ash
- • Red or purple candle (colors associated with the fire element)
- • Photographs of loved ones who have departed
- • Red and/or purple cloth
- • Mementos

PREPARING YOUR SHRINE

Step 1 The location of the shrine is best if placed in a south-facing direction. If this isn't possible in your space, put it where it works best for you. The very first time you build your shrine, ask permission to create it, and set your intentions. You do this by saying:

Ancestors/Spirit, I am creating this shrine to acknowledge you and to invite ancestral support, wisdom, and guidance into my daily life.

Step 2 Use ceremonial sage to smudge the room and the area where you are going to create the shrine. Smudge in a clockwise direction and imagine purifying the space to invite your ancestors to come. In that sense, it's like cleaning your house before relatives come over to share connection and a meal you have prepared.

Step 3 After smudging, take sacred ash (from a wood fire or incense stick) that you have prepared or have been given to mark the shrine area. Sprinkle this in a clockwise direction once around the perimeter of your shrine to seal your intention. You just need enough ash to make the circle; it doesn't have to be thick; it just has to go around the area. You do not have to do this every time, only when you feel you need to rededicate the shrine or recommit to your practice. Should you decide to move it to another location, or physically move to a new home, you must dismantle the shrine ritualistically in reverse by sprinkling ash around the shrine in a counterclockwise direction, thanking the space and expressing gratitude to the ancestors, explaining to them why you are changing their location. Start again from the beginning when you set up the new shrine in its new place.

Step 4 Once the shrine space is created, place a candle (red or purple for fire) on the surface to set the intention of working with your shrine. Say a prayer to call in your ancestors and let them know you are ready to communicate with them. An example of a prayer would be:

> *I call upon all of my ancestors that have come before me, who know me the best, and know what I need the most to help me to move forward in this life. May this shrine awaken my light, my fire, my passion, and my purpose. May it be a place I can commune with Spirit to ask for support and guidance. Knowing you are with me, may I hear your guidance more clearly, connect more deeply, and feel your warmth more closely. Together may we heal the traumas of past generations, so I may surrender and align with my calling in the best way for myself, the children, and this world. Ashé.*

Step 5 Place photographs, mementos, and objects that connect you to your ancestors on your shrine:

- Definitely use pictures of your relatives and dear friends. You can also choose from the collection of universal ancestors, anyone who has lived and died, such as historical figures, spiritual leaders, and people you've admired. If you are drawn to anyone in particular, you've got yourself an ancestor and guide that you can include on your shrine. Sobonfu instructed me to put my matriarchal lineage on one side of the shrine and my patriarchal lineage on the other but, don't worry, sometimes it gets hard to do that, so do the best you can. See the picture below for an example. Don't include pictures of anyone who is still living. You don't want to put them on your ancestor shrine! They aren't dead, they are not spirit yet.

- You can also include objects or mementos that remind you of someone special to you, like a flea market hair comb you purchased on that sunny Saturday in 1993 that you spent with your mom or a vase of your grandmother's favorite magnolia blossoms.

Once you've arranged your shrine, light the candle or candles. Imagine igniting your inner light as you connect with the spirit of your ancestors and the element of fire. Spend time with your ancestors and Fire Spirit every day if possible. The goal is to create intimacy with your Spirit people.

Remember, you have chosen these ancestors to help you in this lifetime. Sobonfu said that everything we came with into this incarnation we chose. Before we come into this world, we are spirit, hanging out, doing our work on the other side. We then get called into an office, the Spirit Office. In the office, we are told why we are being chosen to go to earth—to do a job that is unique and only we can do. We are even told how difficult and challenging our lives will be. Despite this, we are excited and confident and sure we can handle whatever comes our way; however, we don't truly comprehend all the hardships we're saying "yes" to, when we accept the call to come to Earth. Just like our human form, we don't listen. Then we land in our mother's belly and life begins. We completely forget the purpose we committed to and the unique mission we were given to perform here. This is the beginning of reconnecting to those spirit guides and remembering our gift to the planet.

PRACTICE: USING YOUR SHRINE

- Start your morning visiting with your ancestors and the fire spirits.
- Grab your cup of coffee or your own morning favorite and spend some time with them.
- Begin with grounding yourself in your body and your space. Breathe deeply and imagine connecting to the earth's core.
- Light your candle so your ancestors know you are ready to get real with them.
- Call in your ancestors and the fire spirits. Tell them what you need, how you feel, why you're there, say hello. Start your conversation.

- Set your intention for whatever you need to talk with them about (some examples: may I feel your warmth as I walk through this day; help me stay grounded today; help me be more creative today). As you do this regularly, you will hear more, see more, and feel more direction. Healing will most certainly open up for you. Your ancestors are still your extended family. And this makes them feel present to you.
- If you don't think you're getting a response, you can say, "Hello! I'm needing your support." Talk with them as if you are speaking to your best friend. You can vent, you can scream, you can cry, you can whine... Maybe you're pissed off at your ancestors. This is a good place to talk to them about how angry you are for whatever is going on with you.
- The point is to be in communication with them daily. To be authentic. To be yourself.

FEEDING YOUR SHRINE: GRATITUDE AND GRIEF

Use your shrine to bring more gratitude into your life. Just put a teaspoon of whatever you're having for dinner on the shrine, or a favorite chocolate bar (replace often). I feed mine usually at every meal, putting it to the side when I go out to eat too. No one usually asks what I am doing and if they do, I just say I am feeding my peeps. This is an act to thank your ancestors for the download they are giving you. And by thanking them, you are asking for more.

SHRINE UPKEEP

Dust your shrine. Clear the plates that you fed your ancestors on daily. Put the food outside for the animals. Windex and oil the picture frames as you would any other area in your home. This is a matter of respect and practicing gratitude. Keeping this energy field clear extends into your own life. Have fun with this. You don't have to be super reverent all the time, because, after all, you are living, and they want to celebrate life with you, too!

Once you begin a conversation with your ancestors, you never know how their communication will appear to you. It could be a message in a song, or your friend calling you at just the right time mentioning something that lets you know that you are being heard. Or, of course, it could be in the form of a driftwood cardinal. It is important to allow yourself to be open to it. It's like building a muscle. Rituals such as these are really like any other practice people do such as meditation or yoga that gets you out of your head and reconnects you with Spirit.

ADDITIONAL FIRE RITUALS

DREAM JOURNAL

Get a journal that you will use every morning to write in and if you don't have a dream just write what you feel upon waking. It will start to awaken the dreams to you. Keep it by your night stand and if you wake in the middle of the night write in it if you can. Immediately upon waking, reflect on what you remember from your dream.

Once you have welcomed yourself to the day, take a moment to write down your dreams, if you remember them. If not, write down how you are feeling about your day ahead. If you wake up feeling fearful, scared, or worried about information you received from your dreams, go outside under a tree and make a small circle with sacred ash from a wood fire or incense stick that you have prepared or have been given. As you make the circle, talk about the dream and how you would like the dream to be changed and to bring peace to you and your family. Take a moment and pray to your ancestors to turn the dream around and bring protection to you and to those you love. Pour a small amount of water in the middle of the ash circle you have created to represent bringing peace to the dream. Then as you come back inside, make a straight line with the ash across the threshold, repeating the prayer to turn around the dream, as well as bring peace to you and your family, adding a small drop of water in the middle of the line that you drew with ash. Of course Sobunfu told me it doesn't always turn around a dream. It may be meant to happen or is to let you know what is coming but when I did this with a nightmare that was about my son, it gave me great relief just by performing the ritual.

CHAPTER 4

Water Element

Water is life.

~ Kono voro

Ice cold watermelon was such a treat during the hot, sticky summer days in Leesburg, Virginia. Granddaddy Hough used to take me for rides in his car during my summer breaks. Whizzing past lazy lawn sprinklers, buzzing mowers, and waving neighbors, I was proud to be with my grandfather, the head of the county water facility. However, the best part of those summer days with him was the watermelon. We even had contests to see who could spit the seeds the furthest. I got really good at it.

In the morning before we would head out on our rounds, my grandfather would plop a warm watermelon in the municipal water tank. At the end of the day, we would head back to his work with the windows rolled down and my legs sticking to the hot seats. By then, the watermelon was ice cold.

Sobonfu always told me I needed water. My African Medicine Wheel chart shows that I am fire all the way through, and I need water as a counter balance. When I ran too fast or got wound up about something, she would remind me to drink water.

"Honey, you need water rituals. Your water needs clearing out and you need to accept these tremendously difficult feelings. Almost everyone would do the same thing as you are doing. In fact, you are doing far better at acknowledging what you feel than most. But you have pushed aside feelings around being divorced, about childhood dreams not being met, about the losses you had, and about the grief you carry from others. It is time to release those feelings."

She would give me small rituals to help me. One of them was a bathing ritual. If ever I needed to slow down before I made an important decision, she would tell me to imagine water pouring through the crown of my head into my body, connecting with the water that flows within my body. She also taught me how to go directly to a water element to pray. I can't tell you how many times I went down to the Potomac River near my home in Leesburg on warm sunny days and on the days when the ice flows were beginning to give way to spring currents. It became my temple and my refuge. To this day, I go to the water when I am feeling restless, or grieving, or grappling with difficult feelings.

Water medicine is very important as it supports how we flow in our everyday world and aligns us to accept our feelings and the information they give us. In this go-go-go world, bringing our water into balance helps us slow down, go with the flow, and dive deep into what our lives are calling us to do.

After getting to know Sobonfu, I came to learn how critically important water was (and is) to her people, the Dagara of Western Africa, because they live in the Sahara Desert. In her village they say, *kono voro*—water is life.

There weren't any wells in the village when Sobonfu was growing up. The task of collecting enough drinkable water was a daily, hours-long chore for women and girls. They walked for hours searching for water and then hours home with the heavy jugs and containers.

"When I finally turned five years of age," she told me, "I was excited to be one of the people who did this important job for my village. I had seen the women and the other girls who were only a little older than me going out together and coming home many hours later, skillfully carrying jugs and containers on their heads. Because I was very small, I started off with a small jug. It didn't occur to me then, that after I got used to carrying it, I would have to carry even bigger jars. Sometimes it took six to eight hours for the whole round trip. One day, when we had already been out for many hours, I was feeling proud of myself carrying my jug. Excited to show my family, I tripped and spilled it all. I couldn't stop crying because I knew how much my village needed that water. It felt like I killed someone by not bringing the water. Someone in my village could die because I spilled water."

One of the first things I did with Sobonfu was to bring her into the local high school and other places where I could gather an audience to hear her talk about her life, her work, and her wisdom. At Heritage High School, in Leesburg, Virginia in 2003, she told the students her story about carrying water as a young girl.

One of my daughter's friends, Kristen Karinshak Wood, pulled me aside after the assembly and said, "Susan, if they have to walk for water, why can't we?" That year, I began Walking for Water, a project through Wisdom Spring, a non-profit organization that Sobonfu started. I have always loved working with teens; water drew me into working with them in a whole new way. I got to see how each one had a gift, and where we could use their gifts to make the dream of bringing water to a remote African village come true. With fifteen teens, Walking for Water organized a 5K walk to raise money to build wells in Sobonfu's village. We raised enough to build five small wells. Today, after 20 years of walk-a-thons, we have raised over $350,000 to build thirty-five wells. That has quenched many thirsty souls!

I thought about all the times water played a role in my life—my grandfather's car rides and the watermelon at the end of the day and my first real job as a lifeguard at the city pool. I loved swimming and, eventually, I became a special needs swim instructor. In the water, I was patient. I was being of service. I flowed. Water led me to my purpose—to help others find theirs.

As I said earlier, water also has to do with grief and grieving. When Sobonfu informed me that the next ritual we would do together would be a community grief ritual, I flat out refused. "Are you kidding?" I told her, "There is no *effing* way people will do a grief ritual as a community. It's hard enough to talk about our grief one-on-one, let alone altogether."

"That is what you and your community need if you want to create a deeper community like a village. You must learn how to grieve together," she responded.

At the time I thought she was talking about a big *effing* funeral. It didn't make a lot of sense to me. I quickly found out that she was just inviting me and the people that were in my community to drop into and accept another level of grief. I hadn't yet lost my parents or it would have been more obvious. In our modern Western culture we don't usually think of grief as a part of ordinary daily life. Having been raised as a Lutheran, we never addressed or talked about our grief. This was a foreign, but intriguing, concept to me. We continued to have this conversation about grief for over three months.

Sobonfu said, "Water is the element that helps us release our grief. This water ritual is one of the most important rituals I bring to the Western world.

It will help you and your community release, cleanse, feel, dive deep, accept, and learn how to work with the grief you carry."

Unsure about this ritual, I eventually agreed to it. Even though I didn't believe I had that much grief, I did want her to come back to Virginia and teach again. If that's what I had to agree to, I would do it. I'm forever grateful that I said yes. Throughout my life, I had practiced individual and group therapies, along with a variety of healing modalities; I had also studied with Buddhist lamas, monks, Native Americans, and Christian healers. My practices led me to many certifications in various modalities, but I can honestly say that eighteen years later, the most important work I have ever done on myself was the grief ritual and its many levels.

I am not going to pretend it was easy. In fact, the first time I experienced the ritual with Sobonfu, I wasn't even sure how I felt about it. It definitely is a courageous process because it isn't easy to talk about the things we hide from others, let alone the things we stuff away and hide from ourselves.

Sobonfu was, of course, right about my having enormous grief that ranged from ancestral grief to personal grief as well as communal grief related to larger events such as 9-11, natural disasters, and mass shootings. Every time I performed this ritual, I found there was still more grief to be released. This ritual allowed me to take the grief and transform it. As time went on, I would look back after each ritual and see how I gained clarity and cleared away debris, allowing myself to honor my pain, transform it, and perhaps most importantly, use it to help others.

One of the main reasons there is so much loneliness, and why we struggle so much with depression, pain, and suffering as a culture, is that we are alone in our grief. In isolation, we believe no one feels like we do. We live in our houses, separated from each other. We are prescribed pills to make us feel better or numb our emotions, or are told to suck it up and be happy. We're asked to move on and keep going. We don't allow time to process, release, and let go of our grief. We pretend we are okay. We devote our time accumulating wealth and status or else convincing ourselves that others are better off than we are. We barely know our neighbors, let alone know how they are feeling.

Sobonfu once told me about a time, when she had just learned to speak English, that a woman asked her how she was doing. Sobonfu began telling the woman that she felt lonely that day and proceeded to talk about her feelings. After a few minutes, she realized the person really didn't want to know how she felt nor did she have time to listen. I'm sure none of us have imagined sharing pieces of our own grief and the person we're talking to is trying real hard to hold back the yawn. It is heartbreaking.

Grief rituals provide the space and time to be held by others and to speak truthfully about how we are doing and feeling. A safe container provides the place to feel nourished and taken in by an individual (or even better, a community), where we can heal and transform with the support and understanding of what it means to be alive. Everything matters.

"No one gets through living on this planet without grief," Sobonfu taught. "When you choose to come to planet Earth, you aren't picking an easy life." Here on Earth, we come to make a difference in the world, and to clean up our shit. No one gets an easy pass. I realized through working in mental health that all people feel isolated. Everyone has suffered significant losses. The more we share our struggles with one another, stop isolating from each other and letting our isolation build up in our own minds, the more we are able to transform and support each other on this planet. I had been taught through other trainings that there were levels of grief. People also believe that some grief is more significant than others. As a result, they refuse to allow what they consider the small stuff to ever be dealt with.

Sobonfu taught that while there are stages of grief, all grief needs to be accepted and understood as natural and, hopefully, grieved communally. There is no hierarchy with grief. At that time, this concept was totally out of the box for me.

"In my village," she said, "when someone dies, everyone from all around comes to grieve. It goes on for three days. People grieve throughout the day and night and you don't even have to know the person to attend and grieve. It is a place to bring your grief about anything, not just about the loss of a person, and listen to one another and share and allow the pain to be. We must have a place to be held and supported in our pain so we can start fresh and have a healthy community."

Once while I was in Sobonfu's village, the elders came to her and said that a man had died from the bite of a puffed adder snake. When this snake strikes a person, they only live for five minutes. The elders felt it would be a good opportunity for us to let go of our grief and participate in this ritual. We would drive to the ritual which would take place an hour's drive by a van from the village. The rest of the villagers would need to walk hours just to participate.

Most of us wanted to go but a few people who traveled with me refused, saying they didn't feel they needed it. This bothered the elders. This bothered Sobonfu. She encouraged them to go, and still some of them refused. Appreciating the luxury of driving and not walking miles in the heat, we could hear the drumming and the beautiful voices as we neared the village. Sobonfu had let the village know we were coming, and they had removed the body of the person who had died so we would not see him as they did. They were afraid that it would be too much for us.

Usually, the shrine that you grieve at in the villages is the dead person sitting in a chair. This is very unlike how we view people in the Western world once they have passed. In the village, the deceased remains naked, not embalmed, sitting in the heat for two days.

I felt this experience would awaken a deeper understanding of what the grief ritual was truly about. I had already experienced grief rituals at home. This was my first grief ritual in Africa. The heat from the bright sun was blistering. The women were dancing their way to the shrine, singing and crying, expressing their feelings and emotions. The beauty of this ritual is difficult for me to put into words. How they moved and the connection they had to their grief carried an energy of release and intense feeling. I had never seen anything like it before or since. It was as if a beautiful story of grief was unfolding before my eyes. Witnessing the ritual awakened my feelings and the sadness of all who had chosen to come. We went to the shrine and started to cry, scream, and yell. The villagers were uneasy about it. They worried about our white skin and whether we could handle the heat. They tried to get us to move back from the shrine, but Sobonfu said, in her native tongue, to let us be as we were. She had taught us the value of feeling, accepting, and cleansing our pain. This ritual allowed us to experience grieving in their community. The singing and connection moved my soul.

Over eighteen years with Sobonfu, I attended at least two to three grief rituals a year. The water and grief rituals have helped me not only forgive myself and others but also witness the beauty contained in experiencing losses. Each loss has helped me become more aware of myself. Through the pain, deep transformation occurred, and awakened the gift that I am here to share with the world. It has taught me another level of feeling, and to open even wider than I previously thought possible.

In the Western world, we struggle with grieving as a culture and as individuals. We are told to suck it up and move on. Yet, in the grief ritual

I have watched people learn how to connect on a deeper level as they share and listen to one another in profound ways. Miracles occur when people gather together and cry. They don't feel alone in their pain. Instead, they find sacredness in building a shrine to bury it.

I have had many people call and thank me over the years for bringing this ritual to them. Some came regularly to the rituals; others came when they had experienced extreme grief, such as the loss of a child. In one instance, a woman walked up to me in a restaurant and told me that without the grief ritual she would have taken her life after her child died. The ritual renewed her hope. While she still feels the painful loss, she now sees her loss as part of her gift to help others who experienced a similar type of pain. This demonstrates the power of the ritual of water where people feel supported in community and share in their sadness, anger, and fear.

Here are several water rituals that may help you move through grief and balance your feelings to find your flow and inner peace.

WATER/RELEASING SHRINE

REASONS YOU USE A WATER SHRINE

- Experience as fully as possible grief, fears, numbness, blocks, conflict, anger, feelings
- Bring balance, clarity, focus
- Ask for rebirth, renewal, restoration
- Receive cleansing, forgiveness, blessings
- Peace, reconciliation, serenity
- Flow, let go, and feel more at ease

TOOLS FOR THE WATER SHRINE

- Smudge
- Ash
- Blue and/or black cloth
- Blue or black candle (colors associated with the water element)
- Blue bowl
- Water

The water shrine is simple and can be placed either inside, using a bowl of water, or outside using a water fountain, bird bath, or water feature. You can also go to a body of water such as a river or ocean or lake to perform this ritual. It can also be used as a forgiveness shrine, a place you can address what needs to be forgiven in your life.

Here are simple steps to make your own water shrine:

PREPARING YOUR SHRINE

Step 1 The location of the shrine is best if placed in the northern section of your home, but never in your bedroom because it is a shrine used to release your baggage. It doesn't belong in your intimate space. If north isn't possible, put it where it will best work for you. Collect your shrine tools before starting and begin by smudging the area.

Step 2 The very first time you build this shrine, you will ask permission to create it, and you will set its intention. You do this by saying:

Water Spirits, I am creating this shrine to acknowledge you and to invite your support and bring peace into my daily life. May you align me with a balanced flow and help me experience and accept fears, burdens, shame, and all types of grief, so that my authentic relationship to what I feel sets up the best conditions for inner peace. May gratitude flow into my daily life.

Step 3 Mark the shrine area with sacred ash (from a wood fire or incense stick) that you have prepared or been given. Sprinkle it in a clockwise direction once around the perimeter of your shrine to seal your intention. You just need enough ash to make the circle. It doesn't have to be thick; it just has to go around the area. You do not have to do this every time, only when you feel you need to rededicate the shrine or recommit to your practice.

Step 4 Lay a blue or black cloth, if you wish, and set a blue or black candle by the blue bowl. Light the candle, this again sets your intention for how you plan to use the shrine. Fill the bowl with water. Now your shrine is activated. And is ready to be used as often as needed.

PRACTICE: USING YOUR SHRINE

Use the water shrine whenever you want to release feelings, need blessings, express gratitude, or ask for forgiveness. The result is always to achieve peace to be able to move through life in a gentler way. Water has many meanings and helps to clean your energy and clarify your path.

Begin by grounding yourself in your body and your space. Breathe deeply and imagine connecting to the earth's core.

Light your candle so the Water Spirits know you are ready to talk with them.

Have a conversation with the Water Spirits, tell them the situation you need to bring peace to. Don't hold back. They are there to help you let loose and feel centered in your body.

When done, thank them for allowing you to let go and to move through your obstacles. Add a pinch of sea salt to the water in your bowl to neutralize the energy and then empty the bowl by a tree or plant to transform the energy you just released.

Unlike the Ancestor shrine, the Water shrine isn't one you keep activated all the time. When you have spent whatever time you need at this shrine, you will want to blow out the candle and empty the water. If outside you will want to periodically clean the water container. If you opt to go to a body of water, keep it simple, just take yourself. Natural water sources are always sanctified. Simply go and pray: pray to discover what's worrying you, what saddens you, tell the water source what you're grateful for and what you need. Speak whatever comes into your heart.

Should you decide to move your shrine to another location, or physically move to a new home, you must dismantle the shrine ritualistically in reverse by sprinkling ash around the shrine in a counterclockwise direction, thanking the space and expressing gratitude to the Water Spirits, explaining to them why you are changing their location. Start again from the beginning when you set up the new shrine in its new place.

ADDITIONAL WATER RITUALS

MILK & HONEY ~ BRINGING IN SWEETNESS AND NURTURANCE

Sobonfu gave me this ritual which has supported me through many struggles and transformative periods in my life. It is meant to occur each Friday after sunrise and before sunset.

1. Place milk and honey in a jar. Milk represents the nurturance that you are bringing into your life; honey represents the sweetness of all life. You will be releasing these substances in water, but before you do so, mix the two together. I shake the mixture together in a jar while speaking and so does everyone else when joining in with me to do this ritual. If you are going to a river, walk with the flow, imagining that you are in your flow and the flow of life. See the water taking this wonderful mixture out into the world. If at the beach, go to the water and let the mixture be taken by the waves.

2. While at the water, give voice and prayers to the elements and to God/Spirit. An example would be to call upon those ancestors as the fire element. This could be Jesus, Grandma, or whoever you feel can support you in the ritual. Those that can help you brighten your light and can bring light into those places you feel are too dark for you to handle alone.

3. Then call in the water. Water, as explained earlier, helps you to let go of grief by acknowledging it. It helps bring clarity to your life and clears the way to awaken you to your flow and helps you dive deep into the flow of your path, your journey. The water will let you float through the events in your life and also supports transformation. Voice what is or isn't working in your life and do your best to give appreciation for all that you have. In this sacred place of water, hand your feelings over to the Water Spirits so they can be heard. Let them cleanse you and help you feel, let go, and start fresh.

4. Ask the Earth Spirits to help you feel at home in your body and to help you connect with the energy of the earth which awakens your heart and aligns you to it. Call in the Earth Spirits to help ground you in this life and in your own body. Ask the earth to awaken you to knowing the love that resides in your heart and the love that is accessible to you because you walk upon this earth. Ask the Earth to reveal your gifts so you can claim them.

5. Then call in the Mineral Spirits which help you to release patterns and awaken you to the real story that helps you to remember the gift of who you are and why you are here. Awaken to the story that you are bringing out into the world both through your community and your own bones that carry the wisdom.

6. Ask the Nature Spirits to bring transformation and help you be your authentic self in the world. Speak from your heart and have a real dialogue with that part of you that needs to voice your feelings of sorrow, of joy, of gratitude. Let it support you in knowing that change is constant and a part of how we grow in this life.

7. If you are in a group, each of you can call in an element in the order above, and if alone acknowledge each one of them. If you struggle with praying to the elements, claim this ritual in your own way. Call upon the highest part of you. It is a way to honor where you are and helps you move forward into a new way which gives you the ability to feel and trust.

I do this in my relationships—with my girlfriends, my clients, and sometimes just with myself and the elements. Every time I do it, I am grateful for the water that allows me to speak my inner truth, my grief, and my gratitude. I don't have to speak it sweetly or lovingly, although you can. I speak it however it wants to come out. It can be through tears, anger, yelling, or yes, sweet expressions. I trust that my Spirit/ancestors/God wants to hear my words and will listen and support my life. I never know how that support will come, but I trust that on Fridays (a day to ground the prayer and be in your heart), I nourish my spirit with my connections to the beautiful water.

Water is life and without water, there is no life. Therefore, I am grateful to take my feelings to this amazing source and feel freer to share the love I have for myself and others. Giving myself the time deepens my connection to myself, to others, and God.

I once did this milk and honey ritual with one of my closest friends by the beach. She thought I was a crazy woman going to the water and letting it rip as I let go of all the shit I had bottled up during the week. A few weeks later, she was joining in with me, freely sharing what was going on in her life. She voiced what she needed and expected from the water and her ancestors. She now lives in France, but does this wherever she is.

DRINK IN PEACE RITUAL

Since we often struggle with sadness and trauma in this life, this next ritual is one you can do daily.

1. After you get up from your bed, take a glass of water and call on the energy of the water to ask for peace to come into your body, your life, your home, your day, and into the world.
2. As you take your first sip of water/coffee/tea, ask to be refreshed, renewed, and prepared for the day. Ask for ease in letting go of any struggles you have or that may come to you throughout the day.
3. Every time you take a drink during your day, repeat the ritual, asking to be filled with peace in your body, your life, your home, and in the world.
4. With each sip, connect with the water and imagine it moving through you, cleansing and awakening a deeper knowing.
5. If you want to take it a step further, thank the water while showering or bathing and repeat the prayer, asking for peace in your body, your life, your home, and in the world.

BATH RITUAL ~ CLARITY/PURIFICATION/RELEASE

This ritual will help cleanse away negativity that clings to you and will alert your deep mind to the fact that some profound change is about to take place. It is designed to work best if performed on four consecutive days/nights.

1. Begin with a clean bathtub.
2. Fill the tub with water.
3. Play relaxing music to put you in a meditative state.
4. Add Epsom salts (it is ok if it is infused with essential oil) or sea salt (non-iodized) to the water.
5. State your intention for purification as you light a candle.
6. Get into the tub. Ask your ancestors, teachers, and spirit guides to cleanse you and purify your heart. Ask for assistance in experiencing whatever it is you need, it can be things like peace of mind, resolution to a conflict, or guidance.
7. While bathing, focus on opening your heart to release anything that no longer serves the highest good for you and your lineage. Imagine breathing through your heart.

8. Repeat your intention ten times. This will more deeply align you with the energy needed for this ritual to succeed. Example: *I call upon my ancestors, teachers and spirit guides to help me let go of _____ which holds me back. I do so with an open heart towards the future and all it holds.*

9. Stay in the tub as long as you are able to focus on your intention.

10. When your mind starts to wander, allow all of the water to drain while you are still sitting in the tub.

11. As the water drains, visualize the negativity and mundane influences that are averse to your intention being sucked down the drain.

12. When the last drop of water leaves the tub, get out.

13. Clean and rinse your tub (this removes negative energy).

14. Shower and towel off while continuing to think about releasing and purifying your heart.

15. To complete this ritual, thank your ancestors, teachers, and spirit guides for their guidance while in the water and for the soul essence that is coming to help you at this time.

SOAP RITUAL ~ LETTING GO OF YOUR EMOTIONS

As you wash your hands, take the soap and imagine you are washing away whatever has gotten you riled up. Set your intention to be with whatever is most difficult and whatever is making you feel stuck. Say, *"Water Spirits, please help me to soothe these feelings that are keeping me in this stuck place. As I cleanse my hands, bring me more clarity so I don't project my struggle onto anybody else."*

CHAPTER 5

Earth Element

Community is the spirit, the guiding light of the tribe, whereby people come together in order to fulfill a specific purpose, to help others to fulfill their purpose, and to take care of one another.

~ Sobonfu Somé

One of my favorite stories from Sobonfu was about a stranger who came to the village when she was five years old. He asked her to get her mother for him. Sobonfu was unsure how to respond because in the village everyone had many mothers and fathers. In fact, she didn't even know *which* mother he wanted to talk to! The concept of one mother or one father was foreign to the villagers.

When Sobonfu asked one of her mothers this question, she was told that there is a mother who gives birth to you. This confused her, so she asked the other mothers. They told her that although they were all her mothers, only one gave birth.

When I heard this story, I was deeply moved by the beauty of this concept and how true it was. Sobonfu also told me that she would go from mother to mother with questions, wanting to hear what each one had to say, and which view she liked the best. I would have loved to have done the same, hearing many viewpoints and then determining which ones worked for me.

The mothers and fathers in the village collaborated to decide how to work with each child. This beautiful arrangement allowed many people to be invested in each member of the village and their children. No one parents alone. Every woman is a mother to all the children, and every man is a father to them. In our Western culture, we don't share our struggles or have others to discuss our issues with or hold us in the best way possible. If we did, we would feel more at home. Instead, we are often lonely and isolated.

The Earth Element is about feeling at home on the inside as well as being at home on the outside. Earth is about love. The Earth Element helps us create an identity in a home where we are nurtured and feel safe. Earth is about mothering, and the value of being mothered. The Earth always holds us.

With increased awareness of the earth and a deepening connection to the Mother, we become more grounded and connected to ourselves. When we feel lost or need to be grounded and mothered, we can connect with the Earth Element and nurture ourselves. The earth continuously feeds, holds, and helps us feel at home within ourselves even when we are not aware of it. We just need to allow ourselves the time to be with it.

I was fortunate to belong to a community where others held and nurtured me, awakening a consciousness I needed. My grandmother lived with me my whole life, and my mother had many female friends. Although I knew that only one was my mother, I felt a unique communal connection with other women. When I had my children, I was open to them being loved by many people. After I met Sobonfu, I clearly saw the value of not parenting alone and the value of community.

Not growing up in an African village, I mothered differently. I had Heidi, a twenty-four-year-old woman, watch over and love my children while I worked. She was, then and now, a true blessing to me.

I met her by chance one day when I was sitting on the stoop outside of my apartment. Actually, I was having a small breakdown. My mom had been helping me raise my then three-and-a-half-year-old daughter, Ashley, alone. It was a lot for Mom to take on at her age. I had searched and found other women who were also raising small children alone. We took turns watching each other's children so that we could each do our jobs. This worked for a time, but my daughter wasn't happy. Ashley was struggling, and I knew it was no longer a good situation for my little girl. I didn't know how I was going to do everything. I was a social worker earning a small salary and needed to earn a living. I felt lost and alone, and I cried a lot. I questioned how I was going to find a good place for my girl and be able to pay for it, in addition to affording our life. As I sat and cried on the stoop, this amazing young woman came out of the apartment.

"What's wrong?" she asked. "What can I do to help you stop crying?"

Heidi had just moved into the apartment below mine. I didn't know her, but I couldn't hold back. I just let it all out, and told her how hopeless I was feeling.

The petite young woman with black hair responded, "Tell me what you need. I can do it."

When she told me she could come up and watch Ashley when I left for work and could pick her up after school, I couldn't believe my ears. And she asked for next to nothing to do this. I was floored at how easily this happened. I had received a miracle. The magic continued from that day on. She was kind and loved my child as her own.

After I remarried and had my son, she continued to help me with both of my children. I felt then, and still feel now, like I had received a priceless gift. I am so grateful that I didn't hide my struggle. If I kept my pain to myself, Heidi would not have been in our lives.

Another woman who became a mother to my children was my friend, Jennifer, an intuitive thirty-year-old woman with curly red hair. I met her at a retreat with Rosalyn Buryere, where we were taught how to channel Spirit by using energy healing. My three-month-old boy, Branner, was with me. When it was Jennifer's turn to receive a healing, she laid on the massage table. I heard an inner voice tell me to put Branner on the table next to her. I knew he was meant to help with Jennifer's healing. I thought, "Why not?" and did as my inner voice instructed.

As Jennifer was being worked on, Branner let out joyful little sounds. Jennifer later told me she heard Spirit say the little boy would always be in her life. She also shared that she didn't know how in the world that was going to happen because she didn't even know me. Jennifer had just left her job as an art curator, and I was working in mental health.

A month later we were at another workshop. We found ourselves connecting on a deeper level. When Jennifer offered to do a reading for me, I quickly said yes. During the reading, Jennifer mentioned two children around me from the spirit world. I was in shock. How did she know that I had lost two children through miscarriages? I instantly felt at peace from the reading because the two children were there in spirit.

Two months later, I brought Jennifer to live in my home one week out of each month to teach intuition to my community. This continued for thirteen years. During that time, she became a part of my family, acting as another mother to my children. Having Jennifer with me one week each month, and my parents living right down the street, I felt blessed with an abundance of mothers.

Jennifer picked me up when I struggled. I couldn't sew a costume to save my life, but Jennifer is a gifted artist, and jumped in to offer her gifts. She also helped with the duties of the house—cooking, cleaning, and errands. She nurtured each child in her special way, and helped shape them into the amazing people they are today.

Jennifer had always wanted children, but two years after we met, she found out she was unable to have them. My family created for Jennifer what she was unable to do for herself—she was a mother to my children and my family was her family. Even though our thirteen years of living together ended, the parenting hasn't stopped. In fact, together, Jennifer and I took each of my children to college and helped them set up their rooms. Today, she continues to play an important part in their lives.

After hosting a ritual weekend in my home, Sobonfu told Jennifer and me that one of the reasons she wanted to teach in Virginia with us was that we were a different type of community. We had created a space where people could gather and simply be themselves. She said it was something that I did naturally.

I first learned about community from my parents. When I was a child, my parents let others move in when they needed help. My cousins spent summers with us. I loved the community they provided and have always believed I am better because of it. Because of these life experiences, Sobonfu's stories about community felt right.

To think that each person is necessary to make others better is still something I believe in and embrace. Sobonfu's rituals and talks, as well as hosting her in my home many times throughout the years, have helped me understand even more deeply about how supporting each other and nurturing ourselves is necessary to keep us in balance. It has also shown me how hard it is in this culture to mother and parent without the support of others.

So many of us are lonely within our homes, feeling isolated and trying to do it all on our own. We have to start speaking up about what we need and ask for support, while also giving our support to others. We may think others will feel burdened if we ask for help or share our feelings, but through ritual and sharing, I have found that others feel this same need for connection.

When I called my sweet son, then 21 years old, to share the news that Sobonfu had died, his response was priceless: "Oh no, Mom! One of my mothers has died!"

In that response, I knew I had done something right, that my son felt as if he had been raised by many mothers, and that he would be able to take his loneliness and needs to others when feeling challenged by life.

Whenever I struggle, I reach out and ask the Spirit world to help my physical friends and me. If I feel lost, I stand on the earth, the mother of all mothers, and ask for support and nurturance.

EARTH/GROUNDING SHRINE

In the village, Earth Shrines were barely discernible to a Western eye. They looked like mounds of dirt. It's only when Sobonfu pointed them out to me that I saw them. Earth is our home on this planet. It gives us a sense of home wherever we go. It empowers and gives us the ability to be seen and acknowledged. It is about nurturing, care-taking, and unconditional love. It provides empowerment, assurance, and reassurance.

REASONS YOU USE AN EARTH SHRINE

➢ Get grounded
➢ Ask for nurturance, self-love
➢ Live from your heart
➢ Empowerment
➢ Helps you see yourself, feel at home in your body

TOOLS FOR THE EARTH SHRINE

• Smudge stick
• Ash
• Yellow or brown cloth
• Yellow or brown candle (colors associated with the earth element)
• Yellow or brown bowl or flower pot
• Dirt

PREPARING YOUR SHRINE

Step 1 The location of the shrine is best placed in the center of your home if indoors. You can also place it outdoors. Collect your shrine tools before starting and begin by smudging the area.

Step 2 The very first time you build this shrine, ground yourself and ask permission to create it. Set your intention for its use. You do this by simply saying:

> *Earth Spirits, I create this shrine to ground me. Help me to be rooted in you so I may be grounded in my own body. Help me align myself with your love so I can love myself. Help me connect with my own heart so I may speak my truth from my heart. Nurture me. Strengthen me. Support me. Open me to your healing energy so I may feel at home within myself and claim my gifts.*

Step 3 Mark the shrine area with sacred ash (from a wood fire or incense stick) that you have prepared or been given. Sprinkle it in a clockwise direction once around the perimeter of your shrine to seal your intention. You just need enough ash to make the circle. It doesn't have to be thick; it just has to go around the area. You do not have to do this every time, only when you feel you need to rededicate the shrine or recommit to your practice.

Step 4 Lay a brown or yellow cloth, if you wish, and set a yellow or brown candle by the bowl filled with dirt from the place you were born, where you live now, or a special place you love. Earth from where you are born is always more powerful, but not crucial if it's not possible to collect. Light the candle to again set your intention for how you plan to use the shrine. Your shrine is now activated.

PRACTICE: USING YOUR SHRINE

1. Use the Earth Shrine whenever you need to get grounded, feel lonely, unloved, or invisible, when you can't speak from a loving place, or are disconnected. Go to the shrine when you need nurturance, when you're not feeling at home within yourself and/or when you want to express gratitude for feeling loved and lovable, nurtured, and supported.

2. Begin by grounding yourself in your body and your space. Breathe deeply and imagine connecting to the Earth's core.

3. Light your candle so the Earth Spirits know you are ready to talk with them.

4. Have a conversation with the Earth Spirits; tell them the situation and the reason you need to bring love and groundedness back into your life. Open yourself to their nurturance. They are there to help you remember that your body is your home.

5. When done, thank them for allowing you to be grounded and centered within yourself and feel love for yourself and others.

Whenever you feel it's needed, add more dirt to freshen the energy of this shrine. You can also make an offering to it when you're stuck or want to give thanks for its work in your life. I like to make a cup of hibiscus tea and pour it into the pot, while praying.

Should you decide to move your shrine to another location, or physically move to a new home, you must dismantle the shrine ritualistically in reverse by sprinkling ash around the shrine in a counterclockwise direction, thanking the space and expressing gratitude to the Earth Spirits, explaining to them why you are changing their location. Start again from the beginning when you set up the new shrine in its new place.

ADDITIONAL EARTH RITUALS

NEW HOME RITUAL

Just before I moved to California, Sobonfu called me and said, "Did you pack the dirt from your childhood backyard yet?"

I said, "No. You never told me I had to take earth from my backyard." While I was born in Leesburg, Virginia, I hadn't thought of taking soil with me to California.

She said, "Don't be so lazy. Get the earth from where you were born. It would be different if it were hours away, but you are right there."

Sobonfu assumed these rituals would not feel odd to this Westerner and said everything like this, matter-of-factly. She explained to me that to feel grounded in a new place, it helps to bring earth from your original home to your new home. You set the energy by mixing the earth where you were born with the earth of your new home to ground the energy and make you feel comfortable in your new surroundings.

Her ritual proved to be far more difficult than imagined for I had been born prematurely in my family home in Leesburg, but it was now an insurance company. To get dirt from that backyard took some planning. It wasn't like I could ring the doorbell and say, "I was born here and need some soil to take with me to California."

My friend, Aimee, who also knew Sobonfu and was a part of my community, joined me on the adventure. Late one night we snuck into the backyard and dug up some dirt. We became dirt robbers!

Sobonfu had instructed me to put earth around the new house. "Put it in the four directions of the property and pray to the earth in gratitude that you have a new home and want to feel grounded and that you are grateful for the home you were born in. Ask for the earth's support as you need its nurturance and love wherever you are.

BODY GROUNDING RITUAL FOR NURTURING AND HEALING

Another ritual Sobonfu instructed me to do when I was going through cancer therapy and didn't feel like I was in my body, was to put the soil (preferably from your birthplace or where you are living) in a low tray or container by my bed. Each night as I went to bed I was to step into that earth. She told me, "Ask the spirit of the earth to nurture your body during the sleeping hours and bring nurturance and healing into your dream time."

Sobonfu said the earth nurtures us always as we sleep. "Bring it closer to you and ask to awaken a deeper healing from the earth."

The earth responds to us when we bring consciousness about how the earth always loves and supports us. Each night I would stand in the dirt for a few minutes and then take a washcloth and brush off the dirt before I got into bed. When I woke up the next morning, I would pull the tray with my earth out from under my bed and step into it again first thing. I would ask the Earth Spirits to bring nurturance into my day and would ask them to heal those parts of me that felt broken and lonely, and to awaken love within me. I would imagine the earth underneath my feet filling me up with love, healing, nurturance, and connection. I would ask the earth to help me feel at home within myself and ground me so I could listen to what my body needed.

You, too, can do this ritual. If you can't get soil from your place of birth, find soil wherever you feel at home and place it in your house or around the perimeter of your land. And whenever you need to feel grounded and nurtured, place soil in a tray and step on it in the morning and before you go to bed.

EARTH PRAYER

For all who walk on this Earth, my prayer for you is not to do this alone. Especially, do not parent alone. The more people who love you and your children, the easier it will be when hardships arise. You are here to walk this Earth together with others, to contribute together, and to change the world and the children of the future, together. May you be filled up with the Earth's energy, and may you step on her gently. Align with her nurturance and bring nurturance to those who need you and your gifts.

CHAPTER 6

Mineral Element

Let us give gratitude for all that happens to us—especially for the hard things, for they are the messengers of potential wisdom.

~ Sobonfu Somé

During my visit to Sobonfu's village, Sobonfu, my friend Jan, and I sat under the only tree in the heat of the day. Talking about the village life, Sobonfu told us, "When you're born in the village, they don't write down anything about your birth. Instead of a certificate, you are given a birth stone."

"Why a stone?" I asked.

"Don't you ever remember what I have told you?" she said. "Stones carry wisdom. They align us with our stories from past lives and with the stories we're to bring into this lifetime." In Sobonfu's tradition minerals (stones, rocks, crystals, and bones) carry the stories of our lives. They are the external representation of the stories and inner wisdom that we carry deep within our bones.

My friend had brought a couple of rocks from the United States to give to the leader of the Mineral Clan. That elder sat across from us under the tree and stared our way. I knew that my friend had her minerals in her pocket. We exchanged glances, as if we both wondered if he could feel the rocks.

Jan had hoped the elder could get the rocks to explain her stories and even the stories of our country. She handed them to him. We sat there for quite some time watching him feel the stones. He turned them over and held them in a way that was loving and curious. It was like watching a story unfold. Not quite knowing what they were telling him, we each had our own intuition about what he was communicating with the rocks. I was fascinated with the elder's ability to do this for such a long period of time. I was surprised I watched as long as I did, feeling absolutely enthralled. According to Sobonfu, minerals help us with communication and creativity. I wondered what the elder was learning about us and what it was like to be a Westerner. That day I was able to witness how stones, rocks, minerals, and crystals, ancient and beautiful, hold an energy that can realign us with our innate wisdom and help us remember that which we can't do on our own.

One lesson that I received from my bones showed up through pain. Pain comes in many different forms. At times it appears in our emotions, and at others, it occurs in physical or spiritual form. If we don't pay attention to pain, it grows and grows, demanding our focus and showing the way to our own healing.

I had always been healthy and athletic. I was a runner and a biker, and I could pretty much eat and do as I pleased. Physical pain hadn't shown up much. However, when I was 47, I developed an excruciating pain in my thumb. I smacked my hand on a door and it felt like it had been hit with a sledge hammer. Over time the pain grew even more acute. My poor thumb started to look as though it were shriveling. I went to regular and holistic doctors, energy healers, chiropractors, massage therapists, and other pain specialists. Nothing I tried helped. The pain remained unbearable. It grew so intense over the next six years that, at times, I would drop to the floor screaming with agony.

During that time, I went to the hospital for pain relief. X-rays showed nothing. I even wondered if I had made it up and was losing my mind. Finally, an orthopedic doctor told me it was actually sourced from my neck. A nerve was vibrating down to my thumb. In the past I had avoided regular surgery, thinking there had to be another way. But at that point the pain was winning, making it hard for me to function in my life.

All of this pain coincided with a very difficult period in my life. I was grieving the loss of my father, coming to terms with my mother's Alzheimer's disease diagnosis, and watching my marriage fall apart. While I had great friends and children, I always believed that this pain was part of my story. I believed that my lesson was to learn how to shoulder the pain in the kindest, gentlest, most healing way possible, and find the meaning within it. When it became too much, I agreed to surgery.

I was hopeful, at that point, that the surgery would end the pain. The doctor declared the operation successful and said that my pain would soon be gone. He had replaced two of my vertebrates with cadaver bones. I remember, as I came out of the fog of surgery, hearing Sobonfu challenge him on his choice: "Why did you put cadaver bones instead of artificial ones?"

A few days later the nerve pain in my thumb returned with a vengeance. It was the same, old pain. I was severely disappointed, but continued to think as clearly and sensitively as possible. Two weeks later, I found a lump on my breast and was diagnosed with breast cancer. I kept thinking: *How could this be?*

I phoned Sobonfu in Africa and surprisingly managed to connect with her. (That, in itself, was a miracle.) She told me that she would ask the elders what they had to say about my situation. She planned to return to the States the following week and would be in touch.

When she was back in California, we spoke on the phone. However, she didn't tell me much about what the elders said about my diagnosis. Usually she told me where I was blocked, what I needed to change in certain areas in my life, or even gave me a ritual to clear the blockage. This time she said little. Instead, she directed me to go to the woods to do a bizarre ritual that made no sense whatsoever. She said, "Do it. And never tell anyone what you did."

Her unusual silence spooked me: In the past, she had always explained the purpose of a ritual and how to pray around it. When she was in the States, we spoke every day. But this time was different. She felt distant and cold to me. I was confused. Clearly, she knew something she wasn't telling me. After my ritual, my intuitive voice told me to go to a local bookstore and pick up a book about cancer. I immediately drove to the store and found the section on cancer. I picked up several books but one in particular said, "Read me."

I had this internal dialogue with myself about why I should read that specific book as it was about brain cancer. I had breast cancer! Then I heard loud and clear from my inner guidance that I must get the book. After I purchased it, I became obsessed with reading it. Midway through the book, the author talked about a doctor who was trying to prove that we can get cancer from cadaver bones. I slammed the book shut and called Sobonfu.

"The elders told you I got cancer from the cadaver bones," I said, "Why didn't you tell me?"

"They told me you had to figure this out for yourself, that telling you could cause you to freak out."

I didn't freak out; I actually felt relieved. When Sobonfu expressed that the elders said that the cancer wasn't mine, it created relief. The woman whose cadaver bones were in my body woke up the possibility that the cadaver bones had created the cancer. Instead of beating myself up and feeling guilty and inadequate, I saw this as an opportunity to change my story. The cancer wasn't mine; I didn't have to bear all this pain in my life, I could transform it! I began to feel less guilty and inadequate and chose to change my story.

I knew that in order to beat this disease, I had to experience deeper healing. The first part involved learning to not take on other people's problems. I realized that I had a tendency to take care of others and put their needs ahead of my own. It was time to open my heart and receive support from family, friends, and the Spirit world.

After my first chemo, I began to lose my hair and I decided to shave my head. Sobonfu decided that, together with Jennifer, we should perform a ritual around the act. She and Jennifer shaved my head with such tenderness, I felt loved and cared for. Shaving my head allowed me to claim my healing and see how the removal of my hair represented a way to release the old stories and find the real beauty that existed within me. That beauty was reflected back to me through the love of my friends who were holding me so dearly during such a vulnerable time. When the shaving ritual was completed, Jennifer spread the hair around the bushes outside my house as a symbol of my rebirth and growth.

The Elders had told Sobonfu that the cancer was aggressive and to take aggressive action. Therefore, I employed conventional chemo and radiation therapies along with alternative modalities and community rituals. The journey toward healing was a zig-zag. My thumb continued to cause me major distress and pain.

During this process, my mother's Alzheimer's was advancing. But oddly, one of the sweetest parts of how my mother related to my cancer was that with my hair gone, she began to recognize me. My mom remembered me in more of my innocence; she recognized her child.

Occasionally, I would remind her I had cancer, and she would just nod her head disbelievingly and say, "Sure you do." Somehow the fact that I didn't have hair allowed her to want to take care of me. She had always been the person I turned to during my darkest times and who helped me when I was struggling. My mother died the day after my last breast cancer surgery. I believe she stayed alive until she knew that I would defeat the cancer.

As I healed, I was able to move out West and start a new life. I still struggled with debilitating nerve pain, but through the help and the wisdom of an orthopedic hand specialist, we were able to discover the root of the problem—it was a Glomus cyst that had eaten through my bone. Through surgery, he was able to finally put an end to my pain and this time it worked. The deep pain helped me shift my story to one I could share with others. My pain taught me the importance of vulnerability and receptivity. I want my story to give others hope that they can change their story. When you open up to the challenging part of your story and respond with grace, it can heal your life.

While walking on the beach with my husband one day, I picked up a rock and felt it in my hand. "I love this rock," I said aloud. This wasn't unusual for me to say, but that rock felt special as if it had been placed there just for me.

My husband took it out of my hand and said, "Let me look at that."

When he examined it, he exclaimed, "The print on the rock matches your thumbprint. This stuff only happens to you, Susan."

I prayed with gratitude that my story of pain had finally changed and that I could begin a new chapter of my life. The blessing of the rock offered me a gift; it was time to recognize the real story of my life. That rock became special to me. I carried it at all times. About a year later, I spent time with Sobonfu at a Letting Go ritual in Asheville, North Carolina. She had asked the participants to bring something that represented a healing that we wanted. I brought my rock, because I *loved* my rock and I *loved* to share the story. The rock had nothing to do with the healing I needed, or so I thought

Sobonfu took me and the other participants to a river on the property where we were staying. When I went to get into the water to receive my healing, I reached into my pocket to take out my rock. It wasn't there. *Impossible*, because I always carried it with me. I became crazed. I took off all my clothes, thinking it got lodged somewhere. My rock was gone.

I told Sobonfu, "Of course I lost my rock. I had become too attached to the story and my ego had gotten involved." I needed to release the rock, so that I could release my control. Keeping that rock was part of my trying to prove that I was connected to Spirit and that I was deeply spiritual. It is natural that we want to soothe our own pain when it feels intolerable. If I held onto the rock, it felt that I would be able to keep pain at bay. When I lost my sacred symbol, I knew that I needed to find a way to accept whatever I was experiencing—the joy, the pain, the uncertainty—everything that life flings our way. I had a chance to change to another story, a story that allowed me to see my own resilience and brilliance rather than relying on an external object for affirmation. Rocks once again showed me my blind spots and the way forward.

MINERAL/STORYTELLING SHRINE

You create a Mineral Shrine to translate the spirit world into physical reality. This is to improve communication. Release patterns you don't want to carry anymore. Reclaim a story or start a new story. Align with the wisdom of lifetimes that reside in your bones. Start a new chapter in your life. This is where you go when you need help to communicate more clearly with those in your life.

REASONS YOU USE A MINERAL SHRINE

- ➢ Remember your gift
- ➢ Tell your story
- ➢ Let go of old stories or patterns
- ➢ Invite in new stories and patterns
- ➢ Tell off whomever is angering, frustrating, hurting, or injuring you
- ➢ Get unstuck
- ➢ Tap into your own wisdom
- ➢ Ask to communicate more clearly, to be heard and seen

TOOLS FOR THE MINERAL SHRINE

- Smudge stick
- Ash
- White candle (colour associated with the Mineral element)
- Bowl
- Rocks, minerals, crystals, bones

If possible, get a rock from your home; the location you were born or grew up, or if this isn't possible, a place that has particular meaning for you. This rock holds the stories and energy of your birthplace. If you can't retrieve a rock from this place, you can use a rock you love. When you create your shrine, you will call in the energy of the rock as well as the spirit of your birthplace. You can also use several rocks or crystals to create a beautiful shrine.

PREPARING YOUR SHRINE

Step 1 Place this shrine in the west section of your home or outdoors. Collect your shrine tools, and as with all shrines, start by smudging the area you've designated for this shrine.

Step 2 The very first time you build your mineral shrine, ground yourself and ask permission to create it. Set your intention for its use.

I call upon the Mineral Spirits. Come be with me. Help me release the stories and patterns that no longer serve me, that cause me to struggle, so I may step into my gifts to know why I am here. Let this be the place where I can speak my truth.

Step 3 Mark the shrine area with sacred ash (from a wood fire or incense stick) that you have prepared or been given. Sprinkle it in a clockwise direction once around the perimeter of your shrine to seal your intention. You just need enough ash to make the circle. It doesn't have to be thick; it just has to go around the area. You do not have to do this every time, only when you feel you need to rededicate the shrine or recommit to your practice.

Step 4 Place your minerals in a white bowl. A white candle is optional, but suggested if your shrine is indoors. Once this is complete, your shrine is activated.

PRACTICE: USING YOUR SHRINE

Go to the Mineral shrine whenever you're ruminating, stuck in a story or thought, when you're struggling to be heard, need to speak your truth, or not able to shift your pattern. Thursday is the mineral day of the week. It's always especially beneficial to acknowledge your shrine on this day.

1. Begin by grounding yourself in your body and your space. Breathe deeply and imagine connecting to the stones and bones of the planet.
2. Light your candle so the Mineral Spirits know you are ready to talk with them.
3. Have a conversation with the Mineral Spirits, tell them what you need. What stories are coming up for you or what story you want to reclaim. Remember this is a place to bring back the wisdom of your lineage and your past lifetimes.
4. Maintain your shrine by occasionally cleaning your minerals. You can also make an offering to it when you're stuck or want to give thanks for its work in your life. My shrine is outside in a container that has a hole in the bottom. I like to pour a cup of hibiscus tea into it to thank the spirits for their attention. Feel free to get creative. You might add another stone that represents what you want to align with or let go. You can also include bones or sand or salt to your offering.

Remember to dismantle the shrine ritualistically if you decide to move your shrine to another location, or physically move to a new home. You will do this by sprinkling ash around the shrine in a counterclockwise direction, thanking the space and expressing gratitude to the Mineral Spirits, explaining to them why you are changing their location. Start again from the beginning when you set up the new shrine in its new place.

MINERAL PRAYER

My prayer for you is this:

May you hear the wisdom of the ancient ones, for they carry the stories of all time. May you align to your true story of why you are here and may you break free of stories that no longer are needed in your life! May these minerals align you to the next chapter that is ready to unfold with ease and grace!

RELEASE AND RECLAIM RITUAL

What story are you ready to release that no longer serves you? What story are you ready to claim? This simple ritual will help you align with the wisdom in your bones. All you need is two rocks. Don't just run out and pick them up. Start to think about a story that creates turmoil in your life.

If you have a story that you keep repeating and want to shift, begin with a prayer. Ask the Mineral Spirits that reside within you and the rocks you have chosen for this ritual to help you release and reclaim. Then take a rock that speaks to you and feels right to help you release and let go, and another rock that will help you reclaim the real story of who you are. Place the releasing rock into your left hand. Ask your bones (your minerals) to connect with that rock. Then ask that rock to gently pull out that story that no longer serves you. Sit with it and let it do its work. Once you feel like it has worked its magic, place that rock down.

Now put the other rock in your right hand. Imagine it connecting to your bones, really connecting so that you are aligning with, and opening to, the wisdom you have learned from the stories that have taken place throughout your lifetime. Ask for the positive wisdom from all lifetimes to align with your bones and your life. After you complete the entire ritual, take the releasing rock outside and give it back to the earth. Keep the other rock to remind yourself that you have shifted a story.

BREAK FREE RITUAL

This ritual helps you get free of a thought or pattern that keeps replaying in your life. If you don't have a geode, you can find one at a crystal shop or even online. Use goggles to protect your eyes and a hammer and possibly a chisel. Start out with a prayer that aligns you to the Mineral Spirits and your bones. Speak to spirit about what you need help with, then ask the mineral/geode that you will soon hit with a hammer to free you of the pattern. Be ready and willing to let go and release. Then smash it and break it open. Give a piece to someone else who can support you or needs your support to change something in their life. Then keep the other piece for yourself as a reminder that you are now free to live your life differently.

JOB INTERVIEW OR IMPORTANT MEETING RITUAL

As you approach the place where you are going for an interview or other important meeting, look around for two small stones along the path to the building. Hold one in each hand. Call in the spirit of the minerals, your guides, ancestors, and the spirits of that land to wake up to the wisdom in your bones. Ask the Mineral Spirits to help you communicate well with clarity. Call on them to help you listen attentively, to hear from a deeper level what the interviewer and you need from each other. And finally, ask for help to accept the outcome, whatever it may be. As you step across the threshold of the outside door to the building, gently drop one of the rocks over your left shoulder. Do not look back behind you or turn around even if someone calls to you until you've completely entered the building. Place the other rock in your pocket or purse until your meeting is finished. When you leave, return the rock to its original place thanking it and the Mineral Spirits for their help and support.

CHAPTER 7

Nature Element

*In many cultures, including the Dagara, the idea is
that you sculpt your face as you live, and each wrinkle
shows a particular joy or pain you have survived.*

~ Sobonfu Somé

This chapter has been the most difficult one for me to write. I realize my first face-to-face encounter with Sobonfu was the most important lesson she ever gave me. I certainly didn't know it then. Actually, I didn't understand the depth of that lesson until I started writing this chapter. Nature is about growth, magic, transformation, and change. It's about taking off your mask and being authentic. In order for me to truly own my gifts, I needed to stop playing into society's expectations, claim who I am, and stop playing small.

That first meeting with Sobonfu started with Jennifer and my picking her up at Washington Dulles Airport. We were both feeling anxious and excited. I had been telling my whole community about Sobonfu, and I knew I had placed her on a pedestal. I felt very insecure, thinking I might not be good enough to meet this woman of such profound wisdom. And I was bringing her to the biggest event I had ever organized; over one hundred people were coming to hear her Friday night talk.

Arriving at the airport, we pulled our car to the curb and spotted her standing in her African attire with a blue-patterned head wrap. She wore a beautiful matching blue outfit, causing her to stand out. We parked and got out to greet her. Jennifer and I tried to be proper, which we weren't known for. Sobonfu acted as if she was caught off guard when she met me. I later learned she thought I would be much larger physically since my energy had made such a statement over the phone.

She wanted to sit in the back seat, so, of course, we accommodated her. During the ride to the hotel where we were staying for the weekend ritual workshop, we made small talk but were subdued. Jennifer and I could be quite full of ourselves when we were together, so our quiet and formal interactions in the car felt very unusual for us. After a few minutes, Sobonfu interrupted the silence and told a story about farting. As she spoke, I glanced over at Jennifer, giving her an incredulous look. What was up with this woman? After a few minutes, I chimed in with a story about my dad who had a weird sense of humor. One time he told me to roll the car windows up and he let out a huge fart, thinking it was funny that he could disgust us with the stinky smell. From that moment on, I realized that I didn't have anything to prove to Sobonfu, I could simply enjoy her for who she was, and I could just be myself around her. After I had taken off my mask, the three of us became more comfortable with one another.

As a member of the Nature clan, Sobonfu and the Nature people are known for their trickster ways. They are usually funny, authentically themselves, and can move through life's changes with ease. When their medicine wheel is balanced, they feel aligned with the elements. Later, as I got to know Sobonfu better, I asked her why she started talking about farting the first time we met.

She said, "You were acting like my shit didn't stink. If you weren't going to be real around me, I wouldn't have come back."

Sobonfu taught me that rituals bring deep transformation and help you feel like you are part of something bigger. As I've written, the main gift she gave me was how she allowed me and everyone else to be our authentic selves.

I never felt judged by her. Yes, she called me out when I messed up, but she just said, "So, you messed up. The biggest thing is what you have learned and what you are going to do the next time."

Knowing there would always be a next time helped me realize that we are always going to have troubles and trials and make mistakes. The biggest lesson is how to transform them. That's what Nature is all about: forgiving yourself and learning.

Sobonfu was always herself, she was who she was. She allowed us to see more of her than anyone else: her sweetness, her sadness, her truth, her anger, and her dark side. She was compassionate and held space for each of us to grow and be authentic. She taught me that being myself was the gift I brought into the world. To be me in all my complexities and allow others to be in all of theirs is what will really transform the world.

Oscar Wilde echoed something similar: "Be yourself; everyone else is already taken." This is exactly why I fell in love with Sobonfu's powerful belief that everyone has a gift. When we align and support each other in being ourselves and show up to help each other grow, magic happens. The world is transformed.

I invite you to model Nature spirit and hold space to allow others to grow and make mistakes. Hold space for authenticity. If we join together in community, anything is possible. This message holds true magic.

NATURE/PLANT AND ANIMAL SHRINE

Nature is the universal element; it's all around us but, especially in western society, it's the element we're most disassociated from. The nature ritual connects us again to that fundamental relationship with ourselves, our magic, our joy, our inner nature. It helps us break cycles. Nature is a catalyst, bringing things forward for resolution. How do you deal with and welcome change? When you are in Nature—just as you are—you are simply your authentic self. These rituals are used to remove your mask to reveal your true self and support you in expressing who you are, your essential self.

REASONS YOU USE A NATURE SHRINE

➢ Transformation and change
➢ Remove your mask
➢ Realign with joy, playfulness, delight; your inner trickster
➢ Help you connect with magic
➢ Grow a deeper connection to yourself, your own true nature
➢ Plant seeds of what you want to grow
➢ Shed things that get in the way of your true nature
➢ Break through to your authentic self
➢ Not being afraid to be yourself and show up more fully

TOOLS FOR THE NATURE SHRINE

- Smudge
- Ash
- Green cloth
- Green candle (colour associated with the nature element)
- Plant, tree, seeds
- Face mask for cleansing the skin

PREPARING YOUR SHRINE

If you decide to have your shrine indoors, place it in the East quadrant of your space, if you can. If you wish, you may also select or plant a tree or other plant in your yard that symbolizes your nature. Make the location convenient for frequent rituals.

Step 1 Collect your shrine tools, and start by smudging around the plant or tree you have chosen.

Step 2 Ground yourself. Invoke the Nature Spirits and set your intention for this shrine.

I call in the Spirits of Nature. The spirits that help me transform and move through changes and challenges with ease and grace. Help me be my authentic self, just as you are always. Remove my mask so I may be seen in my authentic essence. May I align with my own inner magic and may I know that magic is always available, even in the most mundane moments. Let this be the place where I can plant the seeds to a deeper connection to my true nature and grow into my best self.

Step 3 Mark the shrine area with sacred ash (from a wood fire or incense stick) that you have prepared or been given. Sprinkle it in a clockwise direction once around the perimeter of your shrine to seal your intention. You just need enough ash to make the circle. It doesn't have to be thick; it just has to go around the area. You do not have to do this every time, only when you feel you need to rededicate the shrine or refocus your practice.

Step 4 Light a green candle if your shrine is indoors. Once this is complete, your shrine is activated and you are ready to commune with your nature.

PRACTICE: USING YOUR SHRINE

1. Go to the nature shrine when you or someone in your life isn't being honest or authentic. This is your opportunity to take off your mask and be truthful with yourself. This is where your inner truth is revealed. It's where you go when you are struggling with challenges and need to make changes that are difficult. Here is where you ask for the support you need to transform and gain acceptance. The nature shrine is also about planting the seeds for what you want to grow in your life. Go here to ask for the support you need to grow: a project, a deeper connection with your inner self, more compassion, or the need to grow in love and joy. This is where true growth lies and helps us to learn how to evolve.

2. Wednesday is nature ritual day! It's always especially beneficial to visit your shrine on this day.

3. Begin as usual by grounding yourself in your body and your space. Breathe deeply and imagine connecting to the nature around you.

4. Light your candle so the Nature Spirits know you are receptive and reaching out to them.

5. Have a conversation with the Nature Spirits, tell them what you need: what struggles are coming up for you or what you want to plant to create a new beginning. Ask for more joy, more play, more love, more spontaneity, more magic, or more serendipity to come to you.

6. Maintain your shrine by keeping your plant healthy and vibrant. If it dies, replace it with a new plant. This may mean that something has shifted and you're ready for a new beginning or some new aspect of you is beginning to grow. If your plant is outside, notice all the changes it goes through each season, as it reflects your own inner cycle. Honor each phase of your life, what needs to be reborn, what needs to be nurtured, what needs to be harvested or shed, and what needs to be allowed to rest. Observe how you can be more attentive and authentic to your needs.

7. Should you decide to move your shrine to another location, or physically move to a new home, remember to dismantle the shrine in the same way as the others. You will do this by sprinkling ash around the shrine in a counterclockwise direction, thanking the space and expressing gratitude to the Nature Spirits, explaining to them why you are changing your location. Start again from the beginning when you set up the new shrine in its new place.

ADDITIONAL NATURE RITUALS

UNMASKING RITUAL

Nature Prayer: *I call upon the Nature Spirits to help me be and see my authentic self. Allow me to take off my mask so that I may align and see the beauty that lies within me and can now be seen by those around me. May I be true to who I am and comfortable in my own skin.*

Nature is just itself. It moves through stages without pause and does its work. Maybe you can call it magic. Consider how the butterfly goes through metamorphosis. This ritual will help you bring a consciousness to noticing when you are masking yourself and when it is safe to take off your mask. In North America, we tend to cover ourselves because we fear being judged and rejected. In the Dagara tradition, being seen for who you are is normal. We are both the light and the dark, but with consciousness it can always be transformed into a positive.

This nature ritual will help you bring awareness to when you are wearing a mask and how to take it off and show your true nature.

1. Buy a face mask product (either wash off or peel off) that you use to cleanse your face.
2. Imagine calling in all of your Nature Spirits.
3. Ask them to reveal your true nature so you can remove your mask and be open to your authentic self.
4. Notice how your face feels before you apply the mask. Ask yourself these questions: What needs to be uncovered? What needs to fall away so I can see myself more clearly?
5. As you apply the product, notice how it starts to tighten your face. Notice where you constrict yourself and stop yourself from being able to be your authentic self, not just to others but to yourself as well.
6. As you peel or wash away the mask, imagine allowing yourself to just be all of who you are.

NOTICE WHAT NATURE TELLS YOU RITUAL

Notice nature's signs and signals all around you as it grows and changes. Allow yourself to open to the possibility that the spirit of nature shows up to give you support on your journey. For example, if a skunk crossed your path, it could mean that you need respect in your life.

– Imagine. Nature is helping you on our journey. Take the time to notice beautiful creatures and plants. They may be your totem which is an animal and/or aspect of nature that helps you. If a butterfly appears repeatedly in your life, google the butterfly totem meaning and see if it holds significance for you. It's important to think about what the animal means personally to you and what it might be trying to show you.
– The same goes for the plant world. You can look up the meaning of a willow tree or the spring flowers and also think about how those spirits make you feel when you see them. This is about starting to trust your interpretation as well as how others see it.

SEED RITUAL ~ WHEN YOU NEED TO SHIFT

Do this ritual when you really need to shift or move stuck energy or want to start something new. This ritual helps you bring focus to attracting love, health, money, and deepening your connection to spirit.

1. First, as always, set your intention. Ask yourself, "What do I want to change?" It can be a new job, a deeper love for yourself or someone else, a new story, a vision, whatever is in the best interest or highest good for yourself at this time.
2. Take:
    ➢ 5 seeds (such as marigold, sunflower, poppy, dandelion, flax, fennel, etc.), pick what feels right to you.
    ➢ 2 grains (ex: rice, millet, barley, beans)
    ➢ Handful of black-eyed peas
    ➢ Honey
    ➢ Leaf or cloth
3. Do this ritual after the sun rises and before the sun sets.

4. Gather the seeds and call in the Nature Spirits and the spirits of the seeds to support your intentions and growth. Each seed has a meaning. You can google them for their meanings or set your own. Set your intention for each seed focusing on what you want that seed to grow as you place it on the cloth or leaf.

5. Pray: *"I call upon my Nature Spirits to help me grow...."*

6. Now that all the seeds and grains are on your cloth or leaf, pour a small amount of honey on the seeds to sweeten your growth. Wrap the bundle of seeds with string if you wish, or simply hold it.

7. Walk or drive to a 4-corner intersection where you cannot see any dead ends.

8. Before you drop your seed bundle, drop a handful of black-eyed peas in the center of the intersection, asking for all obstacles to be removed so you may grow what you desire to grow. Follow with the bundle of seeds.

9. Do not look back in your rearview or turn around or go back through the intersection once you've dropped your bundle.

WEEDING YOUR GARDEN

If you feel overwhelmed or need clarity in a situation, go into the garden and weed as if you're working through the problem. Ask spirit for guidance and direction.

CHAPTER 8

Walk with Endings

Losing someone we love can be an initiation into major life changes. It is not going to be the same again. All our relations with other people and ourselves are forced to shift. We become a new person. Although a part of our heart breaks, the spirit of the departed remains. Through that spirit love continues to flow, helping to show us the way, if we allow it, to the higher states of grace and wisdom we were born to reach.

~ Sobonfu Somè

Before Sobonfu went back to visit her village in Burkina Faso, something she did every winter, she would always come and see me. A few days before her final trip in November 2016, she looked ready to burst. She had been sick for the previous seven years. At first her belly bloated as if she were a few months pregnant, gradually continuing to expand as if she were carrying triplets and then quintuplets.

Over time her energy began to fail, and she struggled to walk. It got more challenging for her to sleep. She had difficulty breathing.

Miraculously, even at the end, Sobonfu's energy would return when she stood in front of people to teach and lecture—so much so that it was hard to believe she was sick—as if Spirit entered and took over her body. She struggled for so long that I came to believe she would recover from the illness that was never diagnosed. It was hard to see her this way. The thought of not having her physical presence overwhelmed me. Though traveling became more difficult, Sobonfu pushed to continue her teaching.

I had traveled with her earlier in the year and saw how much she struggled. I couldn't imagine how she would manage to travel to her village in Burkina Faso. Unstoppable, she headed back to Africa on Election Day, November 2, 2016. She called me from Europe to commiserate, "Oh honey, I am so sorry about the election." I spoke to her several times while she was in Ouagadougou, the capital of Burkina Faso.

Then in January 2017, she called me on her cell phone from the village. "I am so glad I can get you on the phone. It is good for us to be able to talk, but I am not so sure it is good for my village." Each time Sobonfu went home, her village had become more modern, both a blessing and a curse. With modern times encroaching on the village, it risked losing its uniqueness and connection to Spirit.

I didn't hear from Sobonfu for over two weeks, which was unusual for us even while she was in Africa. I worried about her, so when I went to bed, I asked for the support of my ancestors and my dream allies. I had my journal near my bed, ready to record any dreams. Those who are part of the Fire clan in Sobonfu's village are the dreamers and the ones who interpret dreams.

In Sobonfu's tradition everyone dreams but the Fire clan is entrusted with being able to dream for the village. If someone had a dream and believed it was meant for the village or needed interpretation, they would take it to the Fire clan who would then offer a ritual to bring clarity, healing, and insight to help the person understand how to use the information for their healing and/or the village's healing.

Before retiring to bed, I set my intention and asked my dream helpers and my ancestors to help me figure out why I was so edgy and sad lately. That night I received the following dream:

I am traveling to meet Sobonfu to take her home after a lecture. She had just returned from Burkina Faso. We are in a huge auditorium. I'm sitting in the middle of the third row, right in front of the podium where Sobonfu will be speaking.

A slew of people surrounds her. I can only see her head. I can't see her belly and wonder if she is healed. I notice an African man sitting to my left. I talk to him psychically. We communicate in a deep way. I want to lean into him but think this is odd. He feels familiar, as if I know him.

I tell him I'm going to the restroom. As I get up, he pinches my ass. I get upset and say to myself I can't wait to tell her about this man pinching my butt. I think to myself I liked him until he pinched me.

I return to my seat and find the man no longer there. Sobonfu walks to the podium with people still around her. I still can't tell if she is healthy or not. The African man is now standing behind me. He reaches around and pinches my forehead on the location of my third eye. I think there is some weird shit going on and can't wait until the lecture is over so I can talk with Sobonfu about it.

I look at her standing at the podium. Our eyes meet. She winks and points her finger at me. She is filled with light and is completely healthy with no distortions and no big belly. She looks like a black Madonna, radiant and full of life. She is healed! I feel gratitude. Warmth rushes over my body.

I woke up and felt the warmth, but only for a moment. Then came the shock. My sister was dead! I screamed and then sobbed, overwhelmed with grief. Even though it was three in the morning, I immediately jumped out of bed and took ash out of my medicine bowl. I ran outside to perform the ritual that Sobonfu taught me when I feared a dream was true or negative or I wanted to change the dream. I used the ritual to try to shift the trajectory of the dream. Sobonfu had told me many times that when reality has gone too far you can't always change the dream, but I needed to try.

Once I performed the ritual, I returned to bed wondering if Sobonfu was dead. Because she was in Africa, I wouldn't hear any news quickly. I moved back into the dream for guidance. I realized that the man in the dream was the Earth elder who I met while I was in her village but had died two years earlier. He looked younger in the dream. I recalled that I sat in the third row. In Sobonfu's tradition the number three is about change and transformation and taking off the mask to see your authentic self.

The following morning, as I prepared to fly back East to talk in schools about Walking for Water, I felt confused and concerned. I decided that when I arrived in Virginia, I would try to contact Sobonfu in Burkina.

During my layover in Chicago, I received a phone call from a stranger. The woman said, "I was on Facebook with Sobonfu's sister. She wrote that Sobonfu had passed away. I knew you were her person and I knew that if I spoke to you, I would know if it was true."

When I hung up the phone, I felt the truth. Devastated, I fell to the floor in the middle of the airport. Overwhelmed with sadness, I had my own grief ritual, without the support of my village. No one was there to help me handle my grief. No one stood behind me, holding space for my grief like we do during Sobonfu's grief rituals. People stared at me and walked by quickly, as if I were radioactive; a typical response to grief in America. I saw profoundly how we struggle in our culture with feelings that live on a deeper level. People are scared of grief. We are isolated in our grief when we are not in community.

My dream clearly showed me Sobonfu had come to me to tell me she had died and I hoped she was healed and herself again. I semi-pulled myself together and made a phone call to Sobonfu's nephew, Bayari, who was living with her in Sacramento at the time. He told me that since I was traveling, he had wanted to wait until I made it to Leesburg before telling me she died. Once I received the confirmation from Bayari, I called my daughter and my dear friend, Jennifer. I could no longer bear holding the grief by myself.

Then a miracle happened. A kind woman approached me and asked if I was okay.

"No," I said. I then told her I had lost my best friend, my soulmate. I had always thought my soulmate would be a lover, but Sobonfu was my soulmate. In fact, she was a soulmate to many. That was the gift she brought to others. When I boarded the plane, I discovered that, lo and behold, the kind woman was seated next to me. It felt like Sobonfu and my ancestors were looking after me to provide comfort.

I landed around 11 p.m. in Dulles airport. I stayed with a friend in Ashburn but got little sleep. I was barely able to get out of bed due to my overwhelming grief. I wondered how to speak about Sobonfu, since the students had no idea she had passed. For over fourteen years I had been doing the Walking for Water project, but now it felt so odd to talk about the walk when all I could think about was Sobonfu and that we would no longer be working together.

Exhausted, I arrived at Heritage High School at 7:30 a.m. I wanted to get the Walking for Water Club motivated to start preparing for their walk that takes place every Mother's Day weekend. Though I was a wreck, I chose to show my vulnerability and grief to these children. I thanked them for saving so many lives. I told them that we would now do these walks not only to bring water and education to the indigenous villages, but also to honor our dear friend, Sobonfu.

The room went silent as I spoke about her village and how we could thank Sobonfu for bringing her ways to us and for making it possible for them to take water to her people. Since this group of teenagers was the last group to actually meet Sobonfu, I spoke about the ways in which Sobonfu had touched our lives. Together, we honored the woman who had inspired us to bring water to those in need and who had reminded us that water is life.

The young people were amazing. I felt their love for me and for Sobonfu. It seemed fitting that I brought the water of grief to them for they readily accepted the grieving ritual. They embraced the fact that water was life.

During the next four days without sleep I phoned and answered calls from people who had been touched and loved by Sobonfu. Every time I would fall asleep, it seemed she would come to mind and say to me, "Others need to hear from me through you."

I was honored and deeply moved by the love she had given to so many and the love she was receiving. I never realized how many lives she had touched. She hasn't left us; she continues to live in us all. She is now my ancestor. She is right smack in the middle of my shrine with my other ancestors. I feed her regularly. If I can't get the information I need, which is rare, I starve her until I can feel her guidance.

Today, Sobonfu still walks with me. I tell her my woes just like I did before. It has taken time getting used to this new relationship. I see her in my dreams and feel her in my heart. I even hear her boss me around and tell me how to lead the rituals. She was always a force to be reckoned with. However, it isn't the same. I miss our phone calls and being with her in physical form. I miss her guidance and her bossy ways. I miss her jokes and her laughter which was contagious. I still cry and wish I could touch her arm and go out and have dinner with her.

Sobonfu once walked with me in the physical realm; now she walks with me in my heart. She lives with me and guides me in ways that have inspired me to listen differently and to trust more. I am grateful for what she has taught me about her people's ways.

I leave you with this message that I received from Sobonfu. Take risks; do something outrageous. Lean in and jump off when you are pulled to make a move. It could be your ancestors telling you where to go and what to do next. Trust your life is unfolding; don't walk it alone. Call in your ancestors to walk with you. Find your tribe, your village of people. Speak your truth. Show your vulnerability. Share your feelings with others, both the sorrow and the joy. Push yourself to live in community.

We must learn how to live together again and honor each other's gifts. We must see that we are better together than alone. Community is what heals us. Rituals align us to remember.

May your walk be filled with people who honor you and accept you for all that you are. May your ancestors ignite your fire and align you with your gifts. You are always better when you are connected and walking with others in this life.

As Sobonfu said, "We are better together than we are alone."

WEAVING ALL THE ELEMENTS

If you discover during your healing journey that there are energies that you need to bring into your life — such as mothering, nurturing, fathering, protection — you can incorporate rituals on a regular basis if necessary, with people that can help bring these energies into your life.

~ Sobonfu Somè

GROWTH RITUAL ~ What do you want to grow in your life?

Sprouting and growing a seed requires a specific set of actions. You must choose the seed and prepare the soil. You need to weed out anything that prevents new crops from growing. Of course you need to tend to the crops as they grow with a regimen of watering and fertilizing. Creating personal transformation in our lives is just like sprouting and growing a seed. It requires intention, awareness of choosing, trusting and having faith, letting go of the past, and exercising lots of patience.

1. To do this ritual, you will need some seeds, soil, and a pot. Find seeds that speak to you and think about if they are easy to grow or not. Questions to ask while choosing seeds may include the following: What climate are you growing them in? Are they going to be indoors or outdoors? Do they need sunshine or shade? Are they difficult to germinate? Do you need to water them daily? Is your earth nutritious enough for them? Do you need to add minerals to enrich your soil? Do you consider yourself to have a green thumb? Are you in fear that you can't keep them alive? Do you see this as a challenge or are you able to trust the outcome?
2. Your seeds require all the elements to grow and flourish. Without balance, it will be hard for them to become deeply rooted and to rise up with strength and beauty. You are just like the seeds. This ritual invites you to manifest what you desire and flourish along with the seeds that you plant. As you tend to your seeds (and to yourself) consider the following questions:

CONSIDER YOUR FIRE

- Is it in balance?
- How much light do you need?
- Are you running too fast?
- Are you trying to make it grow too quickly?
- Are you giving it the nourishment and time it needs?

CONSIDER YOUR WATER

Every growth needs watering. Water helps you to feel, to bring peace into your life, to let go, and to clear the way for new growth. As you water your plant, think about what *you* need.

- Do you feel stuck?
- Do you need peace? Clarity?
- Imagine the water you are giving your plant moving through you and bringing you what you need.

CONSIDER YOUR EARTH

Think about nourishing your own body.

- Are you grounded?
- What type of nourishment do you need?
- When you are planting the seed and touching the earth, think about what you need for *your* earth to be in balance.

CONSIDER YOUR MINERAL

- Do you need to add rocks to the soil for this seed to grow in the best way possible?
- Do you need more space in your life to let things breathe?
- Are you growing a new story or clearing out an old one?

CONSIDER YOUR NATURE

Take the time to sit with your growth. As your seed grows into a plant, spend time watching the growth and equating it to what is growing in your life. A seed doesn't grow overnight and neither does transformation happen that fast.

- Realize you have the power to determine what grows and how you want it to grow in your garden. You also get to choose how to weed through it.

DAGARA MEDICINE WHEEL

This workbook will help you connect fully with your unique gifts and your own true nature using the elements of the Dagara cosmology. In the Dagara community, you are born into a "clan" depending on the last number of your birth year:

If you were born in a year ending in 2 or 7 you belong to the FIRE CLAN.
If you were born in a year ending in 1 or 6 you belong to the WATER CLAN.
If you were born in a year ending in 0 or 5 you belong to the EARTH CLAN.
If you were born in a year ending in 4 or 9 you belong to the MINERAL CLAN.
If you were born in a year ending in 3 or 8 you belong to the NATURE CLAN.

Everyone has all of the elements within them, but the year they are born determines the clan that heals and works with them more closely.

In the village, each clan supports the community by helping them understand the energy of the elements. This means when someone or a group of people are struggling with a specific issue or disconnection, they go to the clan that holds the energy to heal that particular situation using rituals.

This is the same for us. We need connection to the elements in order to balance our lives and bring forth our gifts. This workbook is a guide to help you awaken those elements within you, and assist you on your spiritual path.

While we carry and we need the energy of all the elements, we work with each element using individual practices to harmonize our lives and wellbeing. Each element has a corresponding day of the week, a finger, a toe, a color, and foods. While these associations are largely a mystery to me, Sobonfu would say they hold the vibration of the corresponding element and are tools to connect with the element, Spirit, and your Higher Self. So when you feel out of balance you can determine which energy you need support from and choose to wear clothing with that element's color such as blue for calm or green for transformation and magic. Or if you need to feel more grounded, eat squash or avocado or meat. If you injure your middle finger, reflect on whether you are feeling your feelings or not feeling enough. Or perhaps you're pissed off and you need to use your middle finger in the correct way.

You can use this workbook in several ways. You may practice each element sequentially, reading and working through the questions provided, or you can skip and choose whichever element speaks to you at that moment. Listen into your intuition, and feel what's right for you.

As a best practice, welcome yourself back each day from what I and others call the dream world as you wake up. Check in with yourself and begin your day with an invocation by calling in the spirits of your ancestors and those guides that know you best and know what you need for the day. Ask them to be aligned with your soul and spirit and to walk with you throughout the day.

Briefly review the day ahead and talk honestly to them about your concerns and the help you need. Spirit is your friend so speak like you would to your best friend. Set your intention to move through your day in the way that best serves you and the world. You may choose a specific ancestor or spirit guide that day depending on how you are feeling and what you are dealing with. Remember that ancestors don't have to be related to you; they can be a spiritual teacher, an ascended master, saint, or someone in history you admire. Think about what qualities you may need for that day and that can help determine who you call in for support.

Pick an element to work with, read the description, and use the questions provided to reflect on how the elements work in your life. Do you need more of the element or less? Or are you feeling in balance? Questions are provided to help you deepen your connection to the element and understand how it manifests within you. Journaling is a great way to get more information on what you need and to think more deeply about what it means to make spirit more a part of your everyday experience. It's not necessary to answer all the questions at once, because that can be overwhelming. Let your intuition guide you. Give yourself permission to do what feels right for you.

Workbook

ALIGNING WITH YOUR MEDICINE WHEEL

FIRE ELEMENT | CONNECT TO SOURCE

Birth Years ending with: 2 or 7
Color: Red and purple
Hand: Pinky finger
Foot: Big toe
Days: Tuesday and Sunday
Direction: South

You use fire in your practice to ignite your passion and burn away what's in the way of your vision and intuition. Fire drives you to do and to dream. Too much fire and you have a tendency to act too quickly, in which case fire needs water for balance. Not enough fire and you procrastinate. Fire allows you to align with your light.

Morning Invocation: Welcome yourself back from the dream world. Wrap your arms around yourself in a hug. Call in your ancestors, teachers, guides, and fire spirits; ask them to help you feel their warmth and guidance throughout the day. Sit with that for a few minutes before you start your day. Write down your dreams, or if you can't remember them, write about how you're feeling about your night's sleep.

Elemental Foods: Ginger, cinnamon, sweet red pepper/paste, cayenne, black pepper, tomato paste, papaya, poultry

FIRE ELEMENT | CONNECT TO SOURCE

Use the following questions to reflect on how the fire shows up in your life.

QUESTIONS

Do you talk to Spirit?

How do you talk to Spirit?

How do you align with Spirit?

Are you honest with Spirit?

When was the first moment you remember connecting to Spirit?

Who supports you in the spiritual world?

Who gives you strength?

What lights you up?

What diminishes your light/fire?

Name five things you feel passionate about.

How well do you remember your dreams?

Do the people you surround yourself with ignite you or diminish you?

Do you experience trouble getting fired up?

Do you burn out on things quickly?

Do people have a hard time keeping up with you?

Do you get bored easily?

ALIGNING WITH YOUR MEDICINE WHEEL

WATER ELEMENT | FLOW

Birth Years ending with: 1 or 6
Color: Black and Blue
Hand: Middle Finger
Foot: Middle Toe
Days: Saturday and Monday
Direction: North

You use water in your practice to help you find your flow—the ebb between what you take in and the ability to release what no longer serves you. Water is all about peace and harmony. Water allows you to feel your feelings. It helps you connect with your feelings and opens you up to what those feelings are telling you. It helps you grieve; moving and deepening your connection with your feelings. If you're stuck in your feeling, water needs fire to move the energy and take action.

Morning Invocation: Welcome yourself back from the dream world. Wrap your arms around yourself in a hug. Call in your ancestors, teachers, guides, and water spirits; ask them for help and guidance throughout the day. When water first touches your body (e.g. drinking a glass of water, washing your hands, taking a shower) ask water to help you foster peace within you and to align you with your feelings to increase your sense of peace and serenity.

Ask water for help releasing negativity and stuck energy. Today is a day of feeling and allowing your flow!

Elemental Foods: Melons, coconut, tomato, water, herb teas, berries, grapes, broth, fish.

WATER ELEMENT | FLOW

Use the following questions to reflect on how the water shows up in your life.

QUESTIONS

Describe the way you allow or don't allow your feelings as they arise.

Do you feel too much? Not enough?

Consider the people you surround yourself with. Are they generally more negative or positive than you?

In what ways do you pick up on others' negative energy?

Are you able to deflect other people's negativity?

How is your grieving process?

What losses do you allow yourself to grieve?

What keeps you stuck?

What do you use to numb yourself out and when do you use it?

What is blocking your flow?

What do you need to release?

When do you feel peaceful?

ALIGNING WITH YOUR MEDICINE WHEEL

EARTH ELEMENT | NOURISH

Birth Years ending with: 0 and 5
Color: Yellow and Brown
Hand: Thumb
Foot: Pinky Toe
Day: Friday
Direction: Center

You use earth in your practice to receive nourishment, the soul food, you need for your higher Self-care. Earth allows you to speak from your heart. Earth is grounding energy. Earth helps you feel at home in your body. It is your connection to your physical body. If you give too much to others, putting their needs above your own, you have too much earth. When you are out of balance with earth you either cannot receive or you're needy. When you are in balance with earth you can give and receive and align to your gifts.

Morning Invocation: Welcome yourself back from the dream world. Wrap your arms around yourself in a hug. Call in your ancestors, teachers, guides, and earth spirits. Ask them for help and guidance throughout the day. When you step out of bed, pause to feel the energy coming from the earth. Allow it to connect and ground you. Imagine your feet sinking into the earth and bringing you nourishment for your day. During the day, eat with intention – allowing your food to nourish your soul.

Elemental Food: Squash fruits (including pumpkin), avocado, red and pink meat, soft cheeses, butter, apples.

EARTH ELEMENT | NOURISH

Use the following questions to reflect on how the earth shows up in your life.

QUESTIONS

How do you nourish yourself?

How do you nurture your well-being?

How often do you practice self-care?

What does your body tell you? Do you listen to it?

Are you kind to yourself? Give yourself examples of how you practice self-compassion.

Do you put others' needs ahead of your own?

Do you feel grounded?

What throws you out of balance?

How have you created walls to protect yourself from hurt?

Do you allow yourself to be imperfect?

Are you able to live in the moment?

Are you able to appreciate your gifts?

How do you manifest your dreams out in the world?

Do you listen to your heart?

What do you do to feel and feed your heart?

ALIGNING WITH YOUR MEDICINE WHEEL

MINERAL ELEMENT | GIFT

Birth Years ending with: 4 and 9
Color: White
Hand: Pointer/Index
Foot: Fourth toe
Day: Thursday
Direction: West

You use mineral in your practice to align with your real gift and the story of who you are. What story do you need to release—what story are you telling yourself, what pattern has you stuck, and beliefs that no longer serve you? Mineral is communication; how we speak to ourselves and others. Mineral is our inner wisdom and all it holds. It's our connection to our bones which carry the stories of this lifetime and all lifetimes. It's also the stories of our ancestors and their wisdom from all times. These stories reside in our bones and the stones of the earth.

Morning Invocation: Welcome yourself back from the dream world. Wrap your arms around yourself in a hug. Call in your ancestors, teachers, guides, and mineral spirits. Ask them for wisdom throughout the day. Stretch your body; feel your bones. Take the time to *really* stretch. On your way to wherever you are going today, pick up a rock. As you feel its weight in your hand, imagine it is aligning to your bones. Remember and connect to its/

your wisdom. If you are struggling with communication, ask the rock for support in being clear and confident in speaking your truth.

Elemental Foods: Root vegetables, lime, shellfish, hard or smoked cheeses, parsley.

MINERAL ELEMENT | GIFT

Use the following questions to reflect on how the mineral shows up in your life.

QUESTIONS

How do you talk?

What is your self-talk?

How do you listen?

Do you listen to yourself?

Have you observed how you are thinking about yourself?

What is your relationship to your thoughts?

Do you find your thoughts more loving or more judgmental?

Do you ask for healing around your self-talk?

Do you seek help to support self-healing?

Do you enjoy telling stories?

Are you a big talker or are you quiet?

How do you use your creative energy? How do you cultivate the artist in you?

What story from your past no longer serves you?

What story now blocks you?

Is there a pattern in your self-storytelling?

What wisdom are you ready to transform and carry forward from your patterns and stories?

Do the people in your life support your growth or hold you in old patterns?

Do you eat enough or too many minerals?

ALIGNING WITH YOUR MEDICINE WHEEL

NATURE ELEMENT | TRUTH/CHANGE/ TRANSFORMATION

Birth Years ending with: 3 and 8
Color: Green
Hand: Ring finger
Foot: Second toe
Day: Wednesday
Direction: East

You use nature to support transformation and change in your life. Nature is about being, exactly as it is. It is about being your authentic Self, your true nature. Nature is mystery. Nature is magic. Magic is the extraordinary in the ordinary that speaks to the human spirit, soul, and heart. Through nature you understand that life is constantly changing. Nature shows you how to move out of your own way and trust. It helps you to take off your mask and connect with joy and your inner truth.

Morning Invocation: Welcome yourself back from the dream world. Wrap your arms around yourself in a hug. Call in your ancestors, teachers, guides, and nature spirits. Ask them for an easy and gentle day. Imagine, as you wash your face, you are taking off your mask. Set your intention to be your authentic self with everyone you meet. During the day, take time to be in nature, bask in the beauty of your surroundings, and breathe in its beingness to sustain you.

Elemental Foods: Leafy greens, celery, basil, mango, egg, nuts, and seeds.

NATURE ELEMENT | TRUTH

Use the following questions to reflect on how the nature element shows up in your life.

QUESTIONS

How do you describe yourself to you?

How would you describe yourself to others?

Are you authentic?

What masks do you hide behind?

When do you wear your mask?

To what extent are you controlling?

Do you like to have people tell you what to do?

When is it hard for you to be authentic?

With whom is it easy for you to reveal your authentic self?

What do you believe magic is?

What does magic look like to you?

What does magic feel like?

How does magic show up in your life?

How do you handle change?

What change have you been putting off?

Do you take time to laugh?

What brings you joy?

How do you bring joy in?

What are you ready to share that it is now time to reveal and heal?

What are you willing to let go of for transformation?

ABOUT THE AUTHOR

Susan Hough has been living her gift for over 35 years. A born healer, she began her journey on the East Coast working with teens and families. The rites of passage of losing her mother, being diagnosed with breast cancer, and suffering through a divorce caused Susan's entire life to shift. Experiencing so many deeply challenging experiences she rededicated herself to turn them into rites of passage which deepened her journey to heal herself emotionally, physically, and spiritually.

Studying the teachings of Sobonfu Somé, Susan felt her life shifting in a new and profound way. After reading Sobonfu's book *The Spirit of Intimacy* several times, she knew they had to meet. When she finally met Sobonfu, they connected on a deep spiritual level, and their lives became intertwined almost immediately. For the next eighteen years, Sobonfu mentored her in the practice of traditional African rituals. Through these rituals Susan expanded the role that spirit plays in her life, and vowed to share this wisdom; creating *Living Your Gifts*.

Susan has the rare perspective of having a background in traditional counseling, studying indigenous healing methods, and training as a life coach. With her diversity of education and experience, she has combined her teachings to develop a coaching practice that honors spirit while integrating traditional methods. Susan's approach to Spiritual Counseling focuses on living your gifts and enabling you to share them with the world. She makes it very clear that to really grow she and all of us need to bring our authentic self forward even when it's difficult.

Susan is a CTI Life Coach, and has trained with Mietek Wierkus in energy healing, Mary Branch Grove in the healing arts, and Jennifer Halls in intuitive healing. She has over 35 years' experience in traditional mental health working with teens and their families. She is also an ordained minister. Susan is the Youth Coordinator and President for Wisdom Spring, Inc., with a fundraising program "Walking For Water," which has placed over thirty-five wells in isolated villages in indigenous communities throughout Africa and India. She has educated over three thousand children and teenagers both stateside and abroad.

For more great books, please visit Empower Press online at
https://gracepointpublishing.com

Made in the USA
Las Vegas, NV
10 August 2021